# CULTURE SHOCK!

## Philippines

**Alfredo & Grace Roces**

**Graphic Arts Center Publishing Company**
Portland, Oregon

**In the same series**

| | | | |
|---|---|---|---|
| *Argentina* | *Egypt* | *Laos* | *Sri Lanka* |
| *Australia* | *Finland* | *Malaysia* | *Sweden* |
| *Austria* | *France* | *Mauritius* | *Switzerland* |
| *Belgium* | *Germany* | *Mexico* | *Syria* |
| *Bolivia* | *Greece* | *Morocco* | *Taiwan* |
| *Borneo* | *Hong Kong* | *Myanmar* | *Thailand* |
| *Britain* | *Hungary* | *Nepal* | *Turkey* |
| *California* | *India* | *Netherlands* | *UAE* |
| *Canada* | *Indonesia* | *Norway* | *Ukraine* |
| *Chile* | *Iran* | *Pakistan* | *USA* |
| *China* | *Ireland* | *Philippines* | *USA—The South* |
| *Cuba* | *Israel* | *Scotland* | *Venezuela* |
| *Czech Republic* | *Italy* | *Singapore* | *Vietnam* |
| *Denmark* | *Japan* | *South Africa* | |
| *Ecuador* | *Korea* | *Spain* | |

| | | |
|---|---|---|
| *Barcelona At Your Door* | *New York At Your Door* | *A Student's Guide* |
| *Chicago At Your Door* | *Paris At Your Door* | *A Traveler's Medical Guide* |
| *Havana At Your Door* | *Rome At Your Door* | |
| *Jakarta At Your Door* | *San Francisco At Your Door* | *A Wife's Guide* |
| *Kuala Lumpur, Malaysia At Your Door* | | *Living and Working Abroad* |
| *London At Your Door* | *A Globe-Trotter's Guide* | *Working Holidays Abroad* |
| | *A Parent's Guide* | |

Illustrations by Shirley Eu
Photographs from Alfredo Roces

© 1985 Times Editions Pte Ltd
© 2000 Times Media Private Limited
Revised 1994, 1999, 2001
Reprinted 1995, 1996, 1997, 1998, 2000, 2001

This book is published by special
arrangement with Times Editions Pte Ltd
Times Centre, 1 New Industrial Road, Singapore 536196
International Standard Book Number 1-55868-627-4
Library of Congress Catalog Number 91-077245
Graphic Arts Center Publishing Company
P.O. Box 10306 • Portland, Oregon 97296-0306 • (503) 226-2402

Printed in Singapore

*To Dr Robert B. Fox,*
*one expat who has contributed greatly*
*to the understanding of Filipinos.*
*May his tribe increase.*

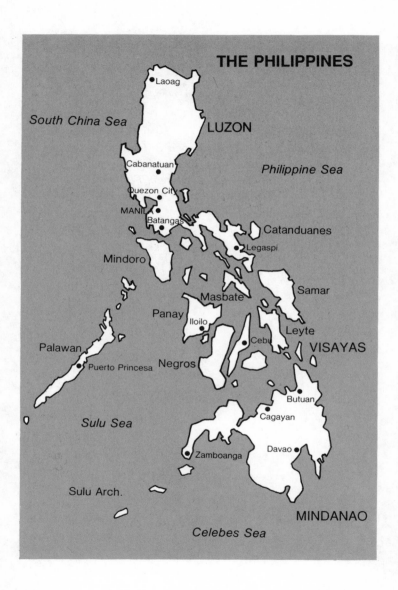

# CONTENTS

5

# ACKNOWLEDGMENTS

*Utang na loob* (or personal favours) is an important social currency in the Philippines. As for us, we have such a debt of gratitude for all the information and insights of a lifetime of living in the Philippines that it cannot be put down in this book. Many people were interviewed and many published sources scrutinized. For very direct assistance, however, we would be remiss if we failed to mention Doreen Gamboa Fernandez, Ateneo University; Jeremy Beckett, Sydney University; Dr Alfred McCoy, University of New South Wales; Mrs Gilda Cordero Fernando, GCF Publications, for valuable comments and suggestions throughout the manuscript stage; Jose R. Sarmiento for providing some photographic illustrations; and Joan Pollett for putting into clear type, a scribble-riddled final draft.

For hard updated data in this revised edition, many thanks to my brother, Marcos Victor Roces, without whose diligent assistance I would still be floundering in the Filipino limbo of vague comments and assurances from all and sundry with no facts and figures at hand; also to Enrique Velasco for advice and comments on the earlier edition of this book; and to business executive Ed Feist for going over the chapter on doing business in the Philippines.

Our *utang na loob* to all who helped, and *salamat po*.

# INTRODUCTION

Most Westerners who come to the Philippines are pleasantly surprised to find all the trappings of the American lifestyle visible—Hollywood films, discos, an English-speaking media with a press fond of American journalistic expressions, fast-food chains, supermarkets, five-star hotels, Christian churches, credit cards. It's all familiar.

A delayed shock follows soon after. The Western visitor may find he is talking the same language, but not communicating at all. With a sinking feeling he realizes he is not in America, or England, or Canada, but in an entirely different world. Feeling betrayed, the Westerner retreats into his own shell, sharing this grievance with fellow Westerners in the safety of private social clubs of particular nationalities.

In other parts of Asia, language, customs and religions clearly establish the difference. Such Asians make no bones about their alien nature; but Filipinos mislead with a Western veneer. In fact, Asians too find Filipinos enigmatic; sometimes Western, sometimes familiarly Asian, always neither one nor the other. Filipinos themselves, in a quandary about their own identity, employ different time frames for Americans (American time), fellow Filipinos and other strangers.

The differences can seem threatening, as newspaper articles accounting how one man kills another for staring at him suggest. Some aspects of Filipino life will probably always remain strange to non-Filipinos. The Westerner puts on a serious scowl and tone when he wishes to make a very important point, whereas the Filipino delivers his most relaxed smile, or even loudest laugh with his vital message. Filipino doctors illustrate this point best. Westerners may be distressed when told they have a very serious health problem from a smiling doctor who appears to be enjoying the telling. This is not callousness, but an accepted bedside manner that seeks to ease anxiety and soften a hard blow. The Filipino laughs, literally laughs, at his troubles; it does not mean he is enjoying himself. This seemingly strange culture has its roots in a dim pre-colonial history, and in Spanish and American colonization. However, the environment becomes less hostile if one can see danger signs and recognize friendly overtures, and manage appropriate gestures at the right moments.

In the Philippine setting, Westerners may find sensing correct behaviour complicated because Filipinos, like most Asians, stress public harmony and overt conviviality. The faintest indication of conflict is readily buried. Direct confrontation is frowned upon and regarded in the worst light. Someone will back off or divert the protagonists. Public conflict is taboo as the ensuing loss of face would lead to wider trouble. The belligerent and aggressive may be feared, but never respected. Failing to see any conflict, the Westerner will miss reading into an incident long-term repercussions. At such highly volatile situations, a foreigner may say the wrong thing, make the wrong gesture and trigger a public explosion which, once in the open, requires vindication of honour or face at any cost.

The colonial experience imposed foreign values that Filipinos adapted or reacted to in their own peculiar fashion. More than three hundred years of Spanish Catholic mores, and fifty years of American free enterprise have reshaped Filipino society, and not necessarily for the better. The contradictions one finds in most societies are therefore more pronounced in Filipino culture.

In the 1960s Filipinos came to realize the need to learn about their own selves; previously they too had believed themselves to be fully Westernized—the only Christian, English-speaking democracy in Asia. Now Filipinos have taken fresh stock of themselves. Behind the Western façade is a unique society. Many aspects of Western culture have been selectively assimilated, adding a distinct dimension to Filipino culture.

This ambivalent character has served the Filipino expatriate in good stead. Filipinos have worked and settled in such remote environments as Alaskan salmon canneries, Hawaiian sugar plantations,

Chicago cocktail bars, Saudi Arabian construction sites, Papua New Guinea banks, Guam business houses, Canadian hotels, Bangkok nightclubs and German hospitals. Unlike most other migrants who still form little communities, the Filipino blends readily into the foreign landscape. He has been called a 'joker' because, like the standard wild card in the deck, he can be whatever he wants to be. Sociologists and Christian theologians, on the other hand, worry about the contradictory moral values Filipinos profess to live by. A Jesuit psychologist discussed such questions in a study with a self-explanatory title: 'Split-level Christianity'.

The elements that produce cultural shock for the foreign visitor to the Philippines are often extremely subtle and microscopic. Only upon their accumulation does the full impact reach the bone.

Filipinos are extremely tolerant people, and thus many grievous social boners will be readily laughed away and graciously dismissed, especially if the offender is a foreigner. Filipinos are generally gregarious, happy, generous people, and it is not difficult to win their friendship and goodwill. Filipino hospitality is almost limitless, and the foreigner, particularly Westerners, are viewed with expansive goodwill. The Filipino has over centuries wrestled with Western culture—its technology, morals, etiquette, organizational systems; he is therefore able and willing to meet a Westerner halfway, perhaps even more than halfway.

The foreigner can remain aloof and an outsider and yet manage to function; but he will be ill at ease. A little understanding and insight will open doors and arms. The expatriate who decides to make this archipelago of more than 60 million people his home, should never take the Western part of the Filipino as the whole. To really know the Filipino, to really feel at ease in this country, it is necessary to probe past the Western veneer, and then an entirely different world reveals itself.

# Chapter One

# UNDERSTANDING FILIPINOS

## A FEW SCENARIOS

### The Gift

You invite Filipinos to your birthday party and they bring presents which you open excitedly in front of them, as is the custom in Europe and America: you have just embarrassed the gift givers. Filipinos consider it bad form to open gifts in public. Those giving are placed in a situation in which the worth of the gift seems to be displayed where other eyes may make a market assessment and compare it to those given by others. Obviously if the gift is materially modest, even if it is the best the giver can afford, opening it would make the thought behind the gift of less significance than its material value.

Opening presents in front of the giver also implies the recipient is avaricious and materialistic, concerned with the substance of the present rather than the act of giving. So do not expect a present you give to be opened in front of you; the Filipino recipient will put it quietly aside. While this appears casual, the identity of gift and giver is mentally recorded. The next time you meet, the recipient may verbally thank you again, this time identifying the item.

### It's Polite to be Late

You are invited to a party in a private house, and as the invitation mentions 7 p.m. you arrive on the dot to find the hostess in curlers and housecoat, distressed at your literal punctuality. You have caught the hosts with their pants down.

It is not regarded polite to be punctual; such prompt appearance makes the guest seem too eager and greedy for food. It is customary to be late; so 15 minutes after the appointed time is being 'punctual'. The more important the invited guest, the later he will make his appearance, as much as two hours later sometimes. Among Filipinos who have studied and worked abroad, punctuality for social gatherings may be practised but this is the exception. However, punctuality for business or official transactions is observed, albeit in a slightly more lax time framework than in the West.

### The Ritual Gesture

You enter the house of a Filipino employee for some cursory business, catch him at lunch, and he invites you to join him. If you actually accept and share the rice and fish on his plate, you will put him in a state of embarrassment and confusion. It is good manners to invite someone to join you for a repast if he chances on you while you are in the midst of a meal, but the expected and proper reply is 'No, thank you, I have eaten.' Similarly if an employee (or even a stranger) enters the house while you are eating, you are expected to extend an invitation out of courtesy but not really to share your meal with the uninvited guest.

## Getting Accepted Gastronomically

These small threads of etiquette cover diverse situations. Filipinos are of course familiar with Westerners, who have been present in the country for over four hundred years, and many Filipinos are well-travelled and therefore aware that a Westerner's ways are different. The outgoing hospitality of Filipinos, along with their willingness to adapt to foreign guests, make it too easy for them to 'be themselves', but then the cultural gap will only be emphasized, and their stay in the Philippines will remain that of spectators and outsiders.

A foreigner who makes the effort to 'get into' the culture, on the other hand, is much appreciated because Filipinos always make a distinction between an outsider, who could even be a fellow Filipino, and one of their particular kin group. When you are offered a boiled duck's egg with a half-incubated chick inside, you will not offend if you decline gently and politely, but you will have missed the opportunity of instant acceptance.

One badge of being Filipino is to partake of a salty paste made of microscopic shrimps; because its overpowering aroma may put foreigners off, Filipinos are delighted no end when they actually eat and relish *bagoong*. A superficial but popular gauge of a stranger's indoctrination into the culture, therefore, is usually the incubated duck's egg called *balut*, and the *bagoong* shrimp paste. It is not necessary to pretend to like those exotic goods, it is enough to be familiar with them and, in true Filipino fashion, smile while gently declining.

# VISITING

## Visiting Friends

1. It is unnecessary to make an appointment for a visit, but it is practical. Do not make a big point of it or people visited will feel they have to prepare something and clean up their house.
2. It is impolite to go into other areas of the house, such as the bathroom, without first asking permission.
3. In rural areas, when entering a house, it is customary to remove your slippers or shoes.

## Receiving Guests

1. Guests are received in the living room.
2. Guests are always served something to eat and drink. If the guest is expected, there must be a specially prepared repast.
3. It is not customary to offer alcoholic drinks.
4. Children are supposed to be seen and not heard. They are usually taken to another room to play among themselves.
5. The host's children, if they are home, come out to greet the adults and then leave the room so they do not disturb the guests.

## Visiting the Sick in Hospital

When friends or relatives are in hospital, it is a duty to visit them, a gesture appreciated and remembered, not only by them but by their relatives, too. Even if your friend is lying unconscious in the Intensive Care Unit, it is still greatly appreciated if you visit the relatives and friends keeping vigil in a hospital, to keep their spirits up.

It is customary to bring flowers or food when visiting sick people in hospital. You will be offered food and drinks by close relatives who are keeping the patient company. They will insist you have a bite before you go as is the case when visiting a friend at home.

## BODY LANGUAGE

The way into Filipino culture is made even more complex by traditional insistence on clouding all social intercourse with a harmonious, pleasant, polite atmosphere. The sooner the foreigner enters this labyrinth, the better, so let us start with the most visible portion of Filipino ways which is, of course, body language.

### Eyebrow Talk

Filipinos greet each other with their eyebrows. Eye contact is established and instantly both eyebrows are raised up and brought down. It is a recognition signal. A smile to go with it becomes a friendly 'hello' without words. An abrupt backward toss of the head with hard eye contact is a challenge, and is usually accompanied by the query: what is it you want?

### Evil Eye

Staring is rude and aggressive. The better part of valour when confronted by a glaring, tough-looking character is to look briefly and then cast one's gaze away. A hard stare has the universal meaning of condemnation (dagger-look), but among Filipinos a fixed eye contact is regarded as provocation. An intoxicated thug, an armed soldier flirting with a girl, will consider your stare intimidation or blatant censure. Parents often control their child's public behaviour by a silent look without angry words, so intense eye contact is a danger signal.

It is also a traditional belief that persons who dabble in occult practices can cause illness by giving one the 'evil eye'. Referred to as *mangkukulam*, these netherworldly individuals are believed to be responsible for all sorts of maladies and afflictions. Do not be fooled by the Catholic exterior of Filipinos. More than 80% of the population is Catholic, but pre-hispanic beliefs die hard, and for many, particularly those outside the cities, a stranger capable of giving an innocent passerby the 'evil eye' really exists.

15

## Obscene Gesture

The ultimate obscene gesture is made with the middle finger pointing straight out, the forefinger and ring finger crooked; though there should never be an occasion for you to use this (belligerence is always generally met with belligerence), at least you will know what someone means when he directs such a finger at you.

## Talking Arms and Hands

Arms akimbo is considered arrogant, challenging, angry. It is not a posture that will win you friends and influence people, unless you are a policeman about to issue a traffic ticket. When a Filipino makes a *faux pax*, he will scratch the back of his lowered head. When crossing a room where there are people conversing, or cutting in between two people talking, hands are clasped together in front and used to advance with lowered head. Another variation used when crossing in front of a person is to extend one hand in front, fingers together as in a karate chop, and with elbow bent and head bowed.

A respectful greeting, particularly for elders or for a godson to his godfather, is to place the elder person's hand or knuckles on one's forehead. While this is no longer seen except in smaller towns and villages, it is still considered the traditional Filipino acknowledgement of respect for elders.

Your attention may be called by an abrupt brush of the finger on your elbow. It is insulting to beckon someone by crooking your finger; the proper form is to use your hand, palm downward. A palm upward motion is rude. Snapping fingers or clapping to call the attention of the waiter is equally rude; you are expected to try to catch his eye and make a slight motion with hand upraised. In desperation you may get away with a soft *pssssst*, but polite society will frown on any loud sounds to call anyone.

Filipinos will point out a direction by pouting their mouths, or shifting their eyes towards the direction indicated.

Mano po. *Traditional greeting of elders. The hand is taken and touched to the younger person's forehead.*

*A light touch on the elbow is commonly used to call someone's attention.*

## *Keeping Your Distance*

There is much physical contact between members of the same sex. Two males holding hands, or with arms over each other's shoulders, are the accepted norm, free of any overtones of homosexuality. On the other hand, physical contact with the opposite sex in public is not on. Ladies greet each other with a kiss on the cheek, but male and female keep respectfully apart. Some women may shake hands with a man, but they have to initiate such a gesture.

## *When You're Smiling*

Filipinos are big on smiles. They smile when they praise, they smile when they criticize; they smile when they are embarrassed and have caused some minor offence; they smile when they need something from you; they smile when they are happy; and for any other reason. A waiter who spills soup on your shirt apologizes with an embarrassed smile; a jeepney driver cutting in front of your moving vehicle smiles in lieu of asking your leave—or is it in triumph at putting one over you? It doesn't matter, the best response in Manila's hopeless traffic tangle, in the broiling noonday heat, is to smile back.

An awkward situation invites a smile because the air is charged with potential conflict and you are expected to smile in return to defuse the situation and clear the air. A smile is a convenient reply when a person does not want to say something unpleasant. Rather than get something critical in words you will get a silent smile. If you ask someone what he thinks about something you just did and he smiles but says nothing, he is not acting the imbecile, he is telling you silently and in the gentlest possible manner he does not think much of it. A smile is the perfect euphemism.

A smile is the best way out of having to say something that could create controversy. Where the Westerner would give a curt 'no comment', the Filipino confronting the media will not budge from his smile. Clearly, there is much to be read into a Filipino smile. With it, subtle mechanisms of social interaction are triggered. There is a smile for every situation; you simply have to learn the meaning by observing the cause and effect of smiles. An accidental pratfall in public will not excite solicitous concern for your safety, but a smile, while waiting to see you stand up and recover by yourself. Verbal concern would only turn public attention to your predicament and cause you loss of face. By deliberately overlooking your public embarrassment while showing sympathy with a smile, your discomfort is supposed to be relieved. One's dignity, or in Filipino-English, 'poise', is always more important than physical calamity.

There are various kinds of smiles and half-smiles, accompanied by eye contact, to cover all occasions. There is no Filipino dictionary of smiles—it takes exposure to comprehend what they are all about. George Guthrie, Pennsylvania State University's Professor of Psychology who studied child-rearing practices and personality formation in the Philippines, has this to say: 'Historically, the Filipino has had little control over his environment. Typhoons, epidemics, invaders or crop failures were to be expected. Smiling and hoping are considered the proper reaction to a situation which is beyond one's control. For this reason one does not show his anger or annoyance when things go wrong. The most desirable pattern, one which is not always achieved, is to keep smiling and create the impression that all is well.'

## Personal Cleanliness

The tropics call for frequent bathing. Daily baths are the rule. A Western visitor to the Philippines in the 1900s, James Le Roy, noted the Filipino being '... scrupulous about his personal cleanliness ... The daily bath is not a luxury, but a habitual necessity for young and old.' They have sensitive noses too. This may puzzle Westerners who will note many public places, particularly marketplaces and slums, giving off decidedly unpleasant aromas, but Filipinos manage to strongly distinguish between public sloppiness and personal cleanliness.

## Flair for Fashion

Appearances are important to a society that values public esteem. One must be stylish. In social gatherings the latest fashion is always admired. People will even overdress at the beach, or for a picnic, enduring discomfort and heat while trying to remain immaculately attired. At the office, business suits, the formal Filipino shirt (*barong tagalog*), or at the very least, trendy short-sleeved shirts are expected of executives. Non-conformity of dress immediately puts a person into the 'outsider' category. Wearing sandals, for example, will classify you as a 'hippie' or a Franciscan monk.

Many office personnel, particularly of government offices or private banks, wear uniforms; this prevents wasteful intra-office competition in fashion while at the same time giving the individual prestige via group identity. Schoolchildren all wear uniforms, so too private security guards. One must try to look like what he is, in the profession he is in and the social class to which he belongs. Fashion designers, referred to locally as couturiers, enjoy social status. Fashion shows are popular events conducted in urban areas, in hotels and nightclubs, and charity balls.

## Beautiful is Beautiful

Beauty contests are even more popular, with every *barrio* (village), *municipio* (town), city and province engaging in the activity. Imelda Marcos, former First Lady and a world celebrity, was known in her high school days as the 'Rose of Tacloban', a town beauty title, and subsequently was involved in a hotly contested Miss Manila contest which had no less than the Manila Mayor intervening and proclaiming her winner. A beauty queen title is recalled when introducing a woman even when she is past her sixties.

From childhood, a Filipina is made conscious of the great social honour of being elevated to the status of a Beauty. The most attractive young girls (or just as often, the children of the wealthiest members of the community) are selected to participate in a religious procession

*Beauty contests are elaborate and popular social events.*

called Flores de Mayo, where they march as *sagalas* and *reinas*, princesses and queen, in Maytime processions in honour of the Blessed Virgin. Athletic teams and social organizations all have a 'muse', one of their members considered the most attractive. It is always regarded as a great family honour to have a member selected as a beauty queen.

An added crown of success for prominent bachelors is marriage or romantic links with someone with a beauty title. Filipinos proudly point out that quite a number of Filipinas have won international beauty queen titles, and that several Filipinos have married foreign title winners of international beauty contests.

## Good Grooming

Focus on beauty as a desirable social asset heightens awareness of good grooming. Beauty refers to more than mere physical pulchritude.

*Former Miss Universe, Armi Kuusela, married a Filipino millionaire and their love story was made into a popular local movie. She was one of Manila's prominent social set, offering advice to beauty contestants entering international competitions. She now lives in the USA.*

A flair for good clothes, for hair-styling, selection of the proper jewellery to wear, posture, poise, and personality; and special talents, such as singing, dancing, playing a musical instrument (traditionally the piano), theatre, speech and declamation, cooking, or certain sports (tennis and pelota), and activity in social organizations involving charity drives, are highly prized.

Appearances refer first and foremost to one's physical appearance, clothes, taste in styling and colour, proper use of valuable jewellery (Filipinas definitely favour fine jewellery over trinkets), social graces, courtesy, and display of wealth and social status. Social gatherings are always abuzz with assessments of apparel and jewellery worn by prominent people. Not too many years ago, various grandiose balls organized by regional social clubs used to be arenas for competitive opulence, until in the 1960s Manila's Mayor Villegas threatened to ban a dance organized by Visayas' wealthiest by charging them with 'conspicuous consumption'. Public display of wealth is toned down these days, but 'conspicuous consumption' lingers as a form of social one-upmanship.

## DATING ETIQUETTE

### Who Pays

The boy is always expected to pay, even if the outing was at the girl's invitation. In a group, the boys may divide the bill between themselves or the whole group may choose to chip in.

### The Chaperone

Some girls will bring a chaperone on a date. The chaperone is usually either a sister, relative or friend of the girl who is approved by the family. The chaperone is almost always a girl. If it is a boy, he would be a relative or friend of the family.

The chaperone goes everywhere with the couple so it is more like a group outing than a date. The boy may bring along a male friend so that it becomes a double date. In practice today, the official chaperone has been replaced by couples going with friends as a group or on a double date.

### Curfew

Many parents set a curfew for their daughters. It is wise to ask the girl if she has one and, if so, make sure she is home by then.

### Permission

Girls usually have to ask for permission from their parents to go out and are subjected to the third degree before it is granted, so do not be surprised when you ask a girl out and she tells you she has to ask for permission before she commits herself. She will also need the details of where you are going, with whom, and what time she will be brought back. (If you are a new suitor, she will need to know who your parents are, what you do for a living, how old you are, what degree you hold and at which school—in order to survive her parents' cross-examination.)

## Kissing
Kissing on the first date is usually frowned upon.

## Matchmaking
Dates are usually arranged through friends and relatives. Filipinos love to matchmake. They are forever trying to match their friends and relatives. Relatives and friends ask each other for dates. Friends will often come up to you and say 'I've got a date for you.' If a young man has his eye on a particular girl, he can get a mutual friend to arrange a date with her. Blind dates are common.

# Chapter Two

# MIND YOUR LANGUAGE

There are more than 70 languages and dialects in the Philippines. Nine of these major languages are spoken by 89% of the population. While they have common roots and certain similarities in sound and grammar, a person speaking one language—say Pampango—will find it difficult to communicate with a Cebuano. Add to this words introduced from Chinese, Spanish and English, and you have a very fine communications mess indeed. The national language, called Pilipino, is heavily Tagalog-based. It is a good idea to learn a little Pilipino; or else the language in your locality.

## *The Filipino English Accent*

English was introduced along with the public school system in the early 1900s and thus, as a medium of instruction in schools, is widely understood. However, Filipinos apply the peculiar sounds of the indigenous language they speak in their locality when pronouncing English words. Few Filipinos will distinguish between the short 'i' sound and long 'e' sound; and 'big' will always sound *beeg*. The mixed 'ae' sound in 'ham' will sound as *hum* to a Westerner. Simply put, Filipinos use vowel sounds as in the Spanish five vowel sounds without the complex and illogical phonetic variation English gives to these vowels.

The inability among many Filipinos to pronounce 'f', which is substituted by 'p' (an example being the national language, which is spelt and pronounced *Pilipino*), is due to the absence of the letter 'f' in Philippine languages. An even further complication is that at times the 'f' sound paradoxically appears in place of 'p'. The inversion of 'p' and 'f' sounds is more marked among the Pampangos, despite the fact that the very name of this linguistic and cultural grouping has 'p' sounds!

The Ilocanos do not distinguish soft 'th' or final 'd' sounds, with the phonetic sounds coming off hard and coarse, 'steek en ooniuns' for 'steak and onions' for example, while Visayans apply lilting musical sounds to words.

Of course once these accents become familiar there are no impediments to understanding, so the point we are making here is that these accents, strange as they may sound at first, do not mean that the Filipino talking to you cannot understand English, or that you should speak pidgin or 'Tarzan' English to him in response. Speaking slowly, rather than loudly, will help as most Filipinos have the impression that Westerners, particularly Americans and Australians, mumble rapidly through their noses.

## *Language Reflects Culture*

The use of language also reflects the Filipino desire to keep himself in low profile while simultaneously seeking to please whoever he is talking to by placing the person addressed in the best light possible. Titles are often used in this manner. It is common to hear a person, say a Mr Cruz, addressed as 'attorney Cruz', or 'engineer Cruz', or 'assistant secretary Cruz', 'architect Cruz', and so on.

Needless to say, public officials are addressed by their office title, such as 'Mr Secretary', 'Director Cruz', 'Monsignor Cruz', 'Vice Mayor Cruz', and so on. Even the wives of such officials are commonly addressed as 'Mrs Secretary' or 'Mrs Mayor'! A wife is often referred to as 'commander', half in jest and half in recognition of her powerful role.

It is not unusual for a mere soldier or policeman to be referred to as 'captain', and a captain to be addressed as 'major' in the desire to give the person addressed greater importance. The practice of upgrading and using professional titles is even applied to waiters and cab-drivers who are at times addressed as 'boss' or 'manager', clearly carrying the desire to upgrade into far-out horizons.

The examples provided, while common, should not be considered a rule for foreigners, as it is sufficient and proper to address persons by their correct titles and positions. What is important for non-Filipinos is to understand the Filipino inclination in language to recognize every person's need for self-esteem. Great care is exercised in language to preserve this self-esteem in public.

The lowliest beggar is given this public consideration in language. A filthy, ragged, and persistently annoying beggar may hang on to you, nudge you with dirty sausage fingers, and pester you endlessly; one is never justified to exclaim: 'Beat it, you bum!' or to say brusquely 'Get out of here.' The Filipino standard reply to beggars is '*Patawarin po*,' literally 'Forgive me, sir.' It is the person who asks forgiveness for not being able to offer the beggar something, not the rude beggar; and he is addressed with '*po*'.

*You will be accosted by beggars, especially children like this one; it is always good form to be polite but firm.*

To show rudeness to a beggar or to someone of lower status will lose you points among those watching. After all, he is just a beggar but you are supposed to be above rude behaviour. A person of high status who is obliging and gentle to someone of lower status (employer to employee, housewife to servant, elder to younger) is highly esteemed. Inversely, rudeness to underlings is considered arrogance for which you get poor marks. Courtesy in language assures the maintenance of overt harmony and a concern for every individual's sense of importance, no matter how lowly his position.

## Filipino English

Some English words have evolved special nuances and meanings. The use of 'D' before a word is popularly used to give names a Frenchified touch of class. Outdoor signs reading D'Pinoy or D'Angel Cocktail Bar, may mystify at first, but it is simply an affectation. The word 'peacetime' refers to the period after the Philippine American War and before World War II (between 1902 and 1941), or simply to pre-World War II days. Most Filipinos like to compare present-day conditions with 'peacetime'. An electric power shutdown in a segment of the city is called a 'brownout'; and treating someone to a dinner or feast is called a 'blowout'.

All Caucasian males are 'Joe' (a hangover of G.I. Joe in World War II) to Filipinos until introduced and a real name substituted. 'Sir' and 'Ma'am' are respectful appellations acquired from American schoolteachers in the early public school system. Thus you may find the househelp saying, 'I have been asked by Sir to give you this' or 'This item was bought by Ma'am.'

Cameras are called 'kodak', refrigerators 'frigidaire', toothpaste 'Colgate', in association with known brands. 'Cowboy' refers to a rough and tough person. Western words like 'cool' and 'dude' are quickly picked up and used to show trendiness and light-heartedness.

## The Cultural Factor

Misunderstandings over language occur less over peculiarities of Filipino English and more because of the deeper and broader social meaning given to terms. Take the framework concerning time which for the Westerner is a ticking digital watch marking off every passing second. Time is less precise in Filipino terms. In the *barrios*, when giving directions to reach a destination, people will measure distance by calculating the time it takes to smoke a cigarette. Since distances in these areas are also seen on a broader scale, the observation 'It is just near by', like the comment 'just a moment', takes in a much longer time span than the city folk's more immediate expectations.

The English word 'fix' has a different cultural connotation. The Filipino who can 'fix' your papers is someone who is a go-between in the bureaucracy, someone who expedites paperwork and even launders illegal transactions, clears tax declaration forms, or disposes of traffic tickets you may have received. A 'fixer' is one whose trade is expediting red tape for a fee. At times his work requires the use of bribes to give your documents a clean bill of health. It is therefore with some care that one should ask if someone can 'fix' your papers for you, or for you to volunteer to 'fix' someone's problem.

Still on the subject of cultural differences revealed in language, it should be noted that Philippine languages are steeped in courtesy. It is important for Filipinos (and Westerners desiring to communicate with Filipinos) not to offend nor to presume anything in speech. Before asking a question of a stranger, say directions to a street or town, one is first expected to inquire if one may ask a question! The proper form is to say: 'Excuse me, may I ask a question?'

The Filipino address of respect is *po* (loosely translated as 'sir' without sexual distinction). This address is applied to strangers, new acquaintances, and elders. In Tagalog, the term 'you' is pluralized when addressing someone to connote respect. The English language being wanting in these formalities, the Filipino is often ill at ease simply saying 'you' to a foreigner he is not intimate with.

## Speak Softly

Never speak in belligerent, harsh or loud tones. Such a speaking style could disrupt harmony, initiate disagreement, and spark off a quarrel. It is therefore not just what one says but the tone and manner in which it is said that is evaluated, that conveys your meaning. Try listening to Filipinos talking, not to what they are saying but to the tone of voice they use, and you will hear mostly gentle and soft sounds; if loud, the sounds are usually boisterous with good humour and laughter. Of course, human nature being what it is, the arrogant, the abrasive, the boastful, are also present; but these readily stand out as dissonant voices. Sometimes one will hear mock angry sounds accompanied by laughter, revealing an intricate and subtle form of getting a critical or negative statement across.

Barking orders and giving public scoldings are improper, all the more so the higher one's office and social position. A firm and forthright tone is only acceptable if one addresses the erring person in private away from the eyes and ears of others.

Various characteristics of Philippine languages further reveal Filipino ways of thinking. For instance, the distinction made in the word 'we': one 'we' including the person addressed (*tayo*) and one excluding him (*kami*). It shows the group orientation of Filipinos. The blackest condemnation directed at someone is *walang-hiya* which means 'without shame' or one who does not know proper behaviour and therefore behaves without any regard for his own self-esteem.

## Filipino 'Yes'

The Filipino 'yes' puzzles most Westerners. A 'yes' could mean just that; but it could also very well mean, 'maybe', or 'I don't know' or 'if you say so', or 'if it will please you', or 'I hope I have said it unenthusiastically enough for you to understand I mean "no".' In his desire to please he cannot bring himself to say 'no' openly. This is why an invitation to dinner has to be pursued and reconfirmed several times, otherwise a casual 'yes' is not deemed binding; the invitation could have been extended as a matter of courtesy; or the person invited and accepting just could not find the proper way to say no, so he says 'yes' to stall, hoping to find the right excuse when the invitation is extended a second time, hopefully through a third person to whom he can say no without qualms.

31

These nuances of the spoken language, including English, reveal the complex Filipino society, one quite different from the recognizably Western pattern of words and sounds that, on first hearing, appears on the surface. It should be obvious by this time that a closer look at Filipino society, and what makes it tick, is essential in order to talk and live among Filipinos.

# Chapter Three

# FILIPINO VALUES

## *The Shame Of It All*

Filipino values have been seriously studied since postwar years; and while important ones have been isolated and identified, there remains no known vaccine against them. You have to live with these values within the society, or at least understand why things may appear to be going wrong while seeming to run a normal course to Filipinos.

The foremost value is called *hiya*. It is the currency applied within the society, controlling and motivating individual and social behaviour.

*Hiya* is shame.

*Hiya* is a universal social sanction, creating a deep emotional realization of having failed to live up to the standards of society. In the Philippine context, anthropologist Frank Lynch, S.J. sees the generic meaning of *hiya* as 'the uncomfortable feeling that accompanies awareness of being, in a socially unacceptable position, or performing a socially unacceptable action'.

Filipino employees tend not to ask questions of a supervisor even if they are not quite sure what they should do because of *hiya*; a host may spend more than he can afford for a party, driven by *hiya*; an employee dismissed from his job may react violently because of *hiya*; a colleague may not openly disagree with you even if he feels strongly about it out of *hiya*. It is a rather difficult word to define. We mentioned earlier that to be charged with not having this sense of hiya is regarded as a grave social sin, and to be labelled *walang-hiya* is the ultimate insult.

Hiya is a controlling element in society. A person's behaviour is restricted by a sense of *hiya* while public behaviour is censured, or approved of, by *hiya*. One's self-esteem goes up and down, depending on the value you place on your own *hiya* in public. To be ridiculed in public, or to be censured openly, or to fail to do what is expected of one, is to suffer *hiya*, a loss of self-esteem. Inversely, not to feel one has acted improperly, to continue to behave in a manner disapproved of by the community, is to be without *hiya*, and this label automatically results in withdrawal of acceptance within one's group, if not the entire community. A Filipino who loses group support from his kinsmen is a social outcast, a very unhappy person. The Westerner who values individualism and non-conformism may find this meaningless because his behaviour is controlled more by individual sense of guilt and less by group censure.

In many *barrios* where more than 80% of the population live, the policeman plays a minimal role, if he exists at all. Community harmony, including all forms of crime control, is maintained by the entire community who resolves disputes largely through a group consensus applying the value of *hiya*. Everyone must have *hiya*, and he behaves in order to win respect from his community.

## A Sense of Self: **Amor-propio**

A pre-hispanic traditional value, *hiya* is reinforced by the Spanish term *amor-propio*, literally 'love of self', in other words self-respect. To accept open criticism meekly, or not to offer honoured guests the proper hospitality, are examples of lack of *amor-propio*. In Philippine society, building up one's self-esteem is essential, and to this end *amor-propio* reinforces *hiya*. The traditional oriental attitude about 'face' comes into play as well in Philippine society, reinforcing *hiya* and *amor-propio*.

Various Filipino expressions reflect the *hiya-amor-propio* syndrome. A person placed in a position where he will suffer loss of prestige, say someone whose son backs out of a wedding after public formalities have been announced, will lament to the son: 'What kind of face can I possibly present before the community if you do this?' (*Anong mukha ang maihaharap ko kung gagawin mo ito?*) A person whose breach of conduct is deemed to have lost him self-esteem or *amor-propio* may receive the judgment: 'His public image is shattered with us.' (*Basang basa ang papel niyan sa amin.*) A literal translation makes reference to one's 'paper' being 'wet', allusions to 'image' presented before the public being 'all wet'.

Sociologist-anthropologist Mary Hollnsteiner states, '*Hiya* may be translated as "a sense of social propriety", as a preventive it makes for conformity to community norms. When one violates such a norm he ordinarily feels a deep sense of shame, a realization of having failed to live up to the standards of society. To call a Filipino *walang-hiya* or "shameless" is to wound him seriously.'

Unlike the Western code of behaviour which hinges on an established code of right and wrong for which an individual feels guilt if he realizes he is wrong, *hiya* operates even when the person

*Public confrontation can lead to violence. Filipinos avoid open conflict—they become a matter of* amor-propio *and honour.*

is absolutely right and the other person wrong, because of the Filipino interaction between *hiya* and *amor-propio*. For instance, to damage another person's *amor-propio* is to invite conflict, even violence; a Filipino is prevented by *hiya* from placing a person's self-esteem in jeopardy. Thus he may hesitate to collect a long overdue financial debt or item borrowed because to bring up the matter face to face may place a person's *amor-propio* at risk.

If you wonder why a Filipino hesitates to bring up a problem, or point out that your slip is showing, or call your attention to an anomalous situation, remember that it is *hiya* in operation. Filipinos feel uneasy if they are instrumental in making waves, rocking the boat, and exposing someone's volatile *amor-propio* to injury.

## The Importance of a Go-between

Face to face situations are therefore avoided or delicately handled because *hiya* and *amor-propio* may come into open play. An intermediary or go-between must step in to keep the situation defused. A go-between makes it possible to bring up matters someone may be embarrassed (*hiya*) to, and the person addressed by the go-between can feel free to turn down the request, or contradict the charges and explain his side without feeling he is, in turn, threatening the *amor-propio* of the petitioner in a face to face situation.

For example, a simple request for a job is fraught with *hiya-amor-propio* elements, since to say a person is not qualified may wound *amor-propio* and cause *hiya* for having presumed to aspire for the job; rejection of an application creates an awkward situation for both the supplicant and the person who has to turn him down. Enter then the third person to convey the request, thus allowing the person from whom the job is solicited to feel free to say no gracefully; rejection is taken in better grace when explained by the intermediary.

The go-between is often used by a young man who wishes to know whether the lady he is attracted to would be receptive to his suit. The way to a Filipina's heart is through her best friend, or a cousin. Given the *hiya-amor-propio* syndrome, where face to face confrontations are totally discouraged, a go-between is indispensable. It is inculcated within the family. Children learn to approach mother over a grievance or disciplinary problems involving father. Grandmother, aunt, sister, brother—all may serve as intermediary over family differences.

The go-between is used in business affairs, government transactions, in dealing with officialdom. In a perverse way, the 'fixer' we mentioned previously (see page 30) is a go-between within the bureaucracy. Lynch observed Philippine society's need for what he termed Smooth Interpersonal Relations (SIR) among Filipinos, citing the role of the go-between. The go-between practice revolves around *hiya* and *amor-propio*, a matter of the highly sensitive self-esteem.

In practical application, business executives dealing with Filipino co-workers and subordinates should be warned that the Filipino value of *hiya-amor-propio* is often the cause of much misunderstanding: As Tomas D. Andres points out in *Understanding Filipino Values, a Management Approach*: 'The Filipino has a high sense of personal dignity. His dignity and honour are everything to him, so that the wounding of them, whether real or imagined, becomes a challenge to his manhood. He respects other people but they must also respect him. Many a conflict between a foreign superior and a Filipino subordinate is founded on a disregard on the one hand, and a sacred regard on the other, of individual dignity.'

## *Euphemism: The Indirect Way*

Aside from a go-between, another way of maintaining smooth interpersonal relations is by the use of euphemism or indirect criticism. One indirect method of criticism is teasing, which, presented lightheartedly, gets the point across, if not the first time, by repetition when picked up by others. It is this reliance on euphemism that makes the Filipino say 'yes' so readily; because he will not openly disagree or disappoint. It is the reason why he smiles so readily even when not agreeing with whomever he is smiling at.

States Andres on this point: 'Foreigners have frequently pointed out that equivocation, "white lies" and euphemistic discourse to avoid unpleasant truths are characteristically Filipino, making an attempt not to embarrass or to displease other persons. The Filipino anticipates and gives the expected answer, avoiding if possible a negative reply. Hence, a question by a person seeking a positive answer concerning, for example, the quantity of payment for services rendered will be invariably answered with "It's up to you".'

Filipinos prefer to say they are not around rather than answer a telephone call or meet a caller with a request they know they will have to turn down. It usually takes longer for anyone in the Philippines to get a proposal turned down because the motions of trying to get it through and of passing the negative judgment to an impersonal committee or some distant powers higher up before the final rejection is very gently and gracefully made are seen to be efforts to prevent a negative action.

Any negative comments, even the most constructive criticism, are prephrased with disclaimers such as: 'This is just my personal opinion, but it seems to me ...', or 'I think it is very good but ...' Sometimes, to ensure negative comments are indirect, they are addressed to a third person or a group, with a pre-warning that if someone feels alluded to he should not be offended, citing a popular saying: 'Falling star from the sky, whoever it falls on should not be offended.' (*Bato-bato sa langit, ang matamaan ay wag magalit.*)

A Filipino may say 'Do I understand you to mean ...' in order to get his criticism across, or 'I think what he is trying to say is that ...' to point out, modify, or add another aspect to the person's viewpoint. He may claim he wants something clarified, to dress up a negative view: 'Please correct me if I am wrong, but don't you think that ...'

## Beating Around the Bush

Foreigners who like to get to the point may sometimes feel mystified by the purpose of a visit to one's office or home to be regaled with light small talk—pleasant conversation that does not justify the call. The caller in the meantime, of course, has been waiting for the foreigner to offer proper openings to discuss the purpose of the visit, sometimes as simple as asking (having established a pleasant climate) during the lull in conversation: 'What can I do for you?'

Often your visitor will not say anything about the nature of his visit and only on the way out, in seeming afterthought, bring up the reason: 'Oh, by the way,' he may blurt out, 'I am in charge of our parish church fund-raising campaign. Would you like to buy some tickets to our benefit show?' or 'I understand you are looking for an accountant. I have a cousin who is looking for a job.'

Some Filipino euphemisms in place of negative comments are: 'maybe' (*siguro nga*), 'if you say so' (*kung sinabi mo ba e*), 'I will try' (*sisikapin ko po*), 'I will make an effort' (*pipilitin ko po*), 'I don't know' (*ewan*), 'We'll see' (*titingnan natin*), 'See how it goes' (*bahala na*). Lifting eyebrows without comment also means 'no'.

On the use of euphemism for smooth interpersonal relations, Lynch concludes: 'It is an art that has long been highly prized in the Philippine society, and is no less highly regarded today. Harsh and insulting words are correspondingly devalued.'

The circumlocution and the time-consuming pleasantries are part of the dynamics of upholding fragile self-esteem. *Hiya* and *amor-propio* require social devices to prevent any damage to precious self-esteem, and harmonious, smooth, interpersonal relations are necessary to ensure this.

The difference between Western and Filipino social interpersonal relations is that Western culture seeks to resolve a conflict by creating confrontation where the Filipino does so by avoiding confrontation.

## *The Art of Togetherness:* Pakikisama

The Filipino expression for what one anthropologist has identified as Smooth Interpersonal Relations is *pakikisama*—meaning, in rough translation, the ability to get along, and implying camaraderie and togetherness.

*Pakikisama* is a desired skill taught to the young; it is invoked to win over a recalcitrant individual to a group's policy to make it unanimous. *Pakikisama* requires someone yielding to group opinion, pressuring him to do what he can for the advancement of his group, sacrificing individual welfare for the general welfare.

In studies conducted among stevedore groups in Manila's docks, Randolph David noted that given a choice between a worker who knew his job but had no *pakikisama* and therefore could not get along with the others, and another who did not know his job but understood *pakikisama*, the unskilled was preferred. Without *pakikisama* a worker, even if skilled, was considered worthless.

## *Debt Cycle:* Utang Na Loob

*Pakikisama* travels on personal favours called *utang na loob*, literally a 'debt of the inner self'. Hollywood's cop-and-robber shows often have police and informers saying 'I owe you one' in reference to favours given; in simplified form this resembles the basic idea of the Filipino obligation to repay a debt on request. *Utang na loob* is more intricate and far-reaching because one is expected to repay the favour with interest, and the fact that one's obligation is not readily quantified creates an escalating cycle of *utang na loob*, weaving a highly complex fabric of interdependence based on *utang na loob*.

Hollnsteiner, in her article 'Reciprocity in the Lowland Philippines' (IPC Papers No. 1, Ateneo de Manila University Press, 1961), observed: 'Every Filipino is expected to possess *utang na loob*; that is, he should be aware of his obligation to those from whom he receives favours and should repay them in an acceptable manner. Since *utang na loob* invariably stems from a service rendered, even though a material gift may be involved, quantification is impossible. One cannot actually measure the repayment but can attempt to make it, nevertheless, either believing that it supersedes the original service in quality, or acknowledging that the reciprocal payment is partial and requires further payment.'

In the circle of Filipino relationships every Filipino has *utang na loob* to someone, while others have *utang na loob* to him. In effect, *utang na loob* binds a group together. A Filipino avoids as much as possible placing himself in such a debt to an outside group, especially a rival or opposing group. It would be disloyal to accept a favour from someone in an opposing group because *utang na loob* creates deep personal and emotional obligations.

The foreigner is best warned before entering this web of reciprocal obligations, as even Filipinos are careful about getting themselves in someone's debt. On the other hand, it is important to understand the workings of *utang na loob* for lack of awareness can cause errors of judgment. For example, a businessman will find that an employee who is less skilled at work and does not appear as conscientious, but who has many friends and relatives in government positions and among business clients may be the most effective because he obviously has built up a bank of *utang na loob*.

## Utang Na Loob *in History*

To further illustrate this point, historians and political analysts claim that the Filipino leaders had been placed in a disadvantageous position in negotiations between the United States and the Philippines after World War II because Filipino leaders acted under a sense of *utang na loob* for the American 'liberation' of the Philippines from Japan. Thus the onerous US parity rights inserted in the Philippine constitution and the re-establishment of US military bases were disproportionate concessions given out of a feeling of obligation to repay *utang na loob*.

A Westerner who gives a Filipino a job, or provides medicine for his hired help's sick child, may receive modest gifts on special occasions such as Christmas, all tokens of recognition of *utang na loob* for service rendered. Professionals, especially doctors and lawyers, are showered with gifts by patients they may have treated free of charge or for a token fee in the past. *Utang na loob* relationships are entered into between parents and children who receive expensive education at some sacrifice from their parents, between poor relations and rich relatives who may provide material help or jobs, between landlord and tenant farmer for a loan of seed or some personal needs, between civil servants and public officials, between colleagues for services rendered without charge, and so on.

Filipino politicians utilize political patronage in exchange for votes at election time, thus introducing the Filipino *utang na loob* element into a Western political system put into operation in the Philippines by the Americans. The political system, from *barrio* level to the national machinery, functions blissfully, largely on *utang na loob*, despite impinging contradictions from theoretical principles and tenets of the Western political model established in the Philippines. The Western model expects the political system to be determined by 'issues', but *utang na loob* has a stronger pull. An ambivalence between the basic Filipino dynamics of power involving such aspects as *utang na loob* and the tenets of democratic elections marks the volatile and footloose Philippine political system.

Therefore, one must be aware that in some diluted form, or even intact in some tiny corner, *utang na loob* as well as *hiya* and *amor-propio* are poised to ambush the unwary person. Smooth interpersonal relations with heavy doses of euphemisms and *pakikisama* always come into play.

## *Kinship Group:* Barangay

The real social unit in Philippine society is the *barangay*, which probably evolved out of the manner the archipelago was colonized by early peoples. Man in the Philippines goes back an estimated 500,000 years, to go by evidence of stone tools in association with fossil *elephas* and other animals discovered in Cagayan Valley. While little is really known of prehistoric man in the Philippines, it is believed that migration and settlement never took the form of some vast city-state under some powerful king or ruler. There are no counterparts to Indonesia's Borobudur or Cambodia's Angkor Wat, nor other evidence of a vast city-state established before colonization by Spain in 1565.

The country was settled by individual boatloads called *barangay* which consisted of a kinship group whose head was called a *dato*. These boatloads settled along the coastal and riverine areas, keeping pretty much to themselves as communities. The Spanish colonizers, who were a mere handful, were able to subjugate a large portion of the country because there was no real unified resistance against them; in fact, the Spanish were able to obtain allies to fight other groups. Rivalry and competition between *barangay* kinship groups were a feature of pre-hispanic Philippine society. In some cases, as among the Ifugao in the mountain provinces, village rivalry developed into head-hunting affairs where the death of someone in a group could only be avenged by the taking of the head of a member of a rival village.

In 1589, a Spanish missionary, Fray Juan de Plasencia, had observed about Filipinos: 'This people have always had chiefs called *datos* who ruled them and led them in war, and who they obeyed and respected ... These chiefs did not have large followings; a hundred households at the most, and even less than thirty. Such a group is called in Tagalog a *barangay*. My understanding of why it is so called is as follows. It is clear from their language that these people are Malays (and hence immigrants); and when they landed in this country the master of a *barangay* (which is properly the name of a ship) must have retained rule as *dato*. Thus even today it is understood that the term *barangay* means originally a family consisting of parents, children, kinsmen and slaves.

'A large number of these *barangays* would form a single town, or at least would settle not far from each other, for the sake of mutual defence in case of war. They were not, however, subject one to another, but bound together by friendship or kinship; and the chiefs, each with his *barangay*, fought side by side in the wars they waged.'

Today, the kinship groups remain very much as in pre-hispanic days with many cultural minority groups scattered in remote areas throughout the archipelago. The basic community unit, called *barrio*, is very much a *barangay* kinship grouping at its core. However, even in towns and cities, albeit in amorphous, adulterated form, the kinship group is alive and well. The Filipino values of *hiya-amor-*

*propio*, *utang na loob* and *pakikisama* function within the context of this kinship group. Filipinos think in terms of the old *barangay* and they identify a person within the context of the kinship group to which he belongs.

## The Kinship Group in Action

*Item:* An American Yale historian doing research in Iloilo discovers some interesting old books and documents in the possession of two ageing spinsters and, expressing great interest, requests permission to study the dusty tomes; he meets with reluctance and suspicion. It takes him six months of persistence before he is allowed to go over the books. He brings a Filipina colleague from Ateneo University who chats with the two spinsters, and after a long conversation unrelated to the books is instantly allowed to examine and read them. Amazed, the American exclaims, 'How did you do that? It took me months to win their confidence!' The Filipina explains, 'I did not show too much interest in the books, I did not even look at the books. First I established my identity in their eyes by saying that I am the niece of someone they know, a friend of another they also know, placing myself in a context of mutual acquaintances.'

The relevance of such casual personal conversation will probably escape the down-to-brasstacks Westerner, but *who* you are can only be perceived by relating you to the kin group you belong to as distinguished from the other person's own kin group.

What anthropologist Dr Robert Fox had to say in 1946, in his published work, *Human Relations Area Files, Inc.*, best describes the Filipino kinship group: 'The basic social unit of the society is the elementary family of mother, father, and children, and the extended bilateral family which includes consanguineal relatives of both the mother and father. The influence of the family permeates all facets of Philippine society. It is the primary unit of corporate action about which social, economic, and religious activities revolve. Religion is family and home-centred to a notable degree. Economic

45

activities, agriculture, fishing, and cottage industries commonly involve all adult members of the family in cooperative labour; often the older children are included as well. The so-called 'corporations' in the Philippines are characteristically family-owned. Nepotism in government and business is widespread, a reflection of family cohesiveness.

'The Filipino family displays great solidarity, emphasizing loyalty and support of the blood group, frequently to the neglect of social organization of broader dimensions such as town or nation ...

'In the typical *barrio* or village, political organization is weakly developed. Group activities are organized on the basis of familial alliance and common economic and ritual interests. Leadership is provided by the dominant family (or families), the primary determinants of the leadership being wealth and the size of the kin group.

'The cohesiveness of the family also has a powerful influence upon interpersonal relationships, particularly with non-kinsmen. An offence against one of its members is interpreted as a threat to the whole family. The family, on the other hand, provides a secure environment for its members, in sharp contrast to the often uncertain and delicate relationships with non-relatives ...'

## What has Kinship Structure to do with Me?

*Item:* An American peace corps worker assigned to a rural area loves to bathe in the river in a skimpy bikini and walk about the village in tight shorts. While hiking by herself in the forest she is sexually assaulted by two men and when she runs back to the village for help, in place of sympathy, the village response is that she had provoked the situation by being a 'Sexy American'.

*Item:* An American scientist has worked out a programme to improve the poultry stock in the Philippines by introducing a fine breed from the United States. At great expense, the exotic roosters are distributed to selected farmers in several *barrios*. The scientist then takes to the field to inspect the progress of the poultry improvement project. Having been informed of the coming visit of so important a personage, one farmer, in keeping with Filipino hospitality, makes preparations to welcome the VIP with the best he could offer. On his arrival at the farmer's house the American scientist is treated to a small feast—and on his dinner plate is the prize chicken, fried. The Filipino host feels only the best will suffice for his honoured guest and, of course, the exotic bird is the best he has to offer.

Kinship structure motivates the Filipino's behaviour. The values previously mentioned very often apply only within each kinship grouping rather than in universal fashion. An outsider is viewed as fair game, and a different set of values is applied to deal with such persons or groups. For example, it is to be expected that a tourist will be charged more than others, but once the 'tourist' has been identified as a guest or friend of someone within the group, the tourist gets a fair price because he is no longer seen as a passing outsider.

*Item:* You are driving along the highway when suddenly a boy dashes in front of you and you hit him. Pick the boy up immediately, take him to the nearest hospital; it is risky to linger in the site as more village folk gather at the scene because in such an emotional atmosphere a mob of kins of the injured boy could get physical. Should you find yourself involved in a road accident, where a mob has started to grumble, it may be better to drive off quickly and report to the nearest police station. *Barrio* folk are of one or two kin groups; they will definitely sympathize with the victim, who is a kin, and resent the outsider.

## Working Both Sides of the Family

The Filipino nuclear family is bilateral; relatives of both husband and wife count equally as relatives, unlike matrilineal or patrilineal societies. To the Filipino kinship group, it is the child who establishes the kinship bond, for the child's grandparents, uncles and aunts, and on down the line, form the common link to both families. Children are important to the kinship group. Among the Ifugao a wedding is usually formalized only after it has been demonstrated the fiancée is bearing a child. In Manila wives commonly address their husbands as 'Daddy' and husbands call their wives 'Mommy', emphasizing their parent status, adjusting their identity to what the child would call his parents.

## Compadrazco: *God Parenthood*

Relatives of course are counted, up to the most distant of cousins. Furthermore, the kinship group expands and grows beyond blood relatives through other rituals, aside from marriage. The Spaniards instituted Christian rites which have been utilized by the Filipino kinship group as a means to extend itself.

The Christian rite of standing as godfather to a child during baptism creates a relationship between godchild and godfather. By strict tradition, a godfather and godmother are considered second parents to the child. They are supposed to make the effort to look after the child should something happen to the child's parents. At Christmas and on the godchild's birthday, it is customary to give a gift. When the child becomes an adult, the godfather or godmother is expected to help the child obtain employment or aid him to get ahead in the world in various ways. However, these ideal expectations are often not put into real practice, though the spirit of providing material support in general is considered a godparent's role. A godfather is called *ninong* and a godmother *ninang* by the godchild, while a godchild is called *inaanak* which, literally translated, means a created sibling, a sibling by ritual.

## *Ritual Brothers are* Compadres

The baptism ritual creates a bond not just between godparents and godchild, but also between godparents and the parents of the child, who then recognize each other as *compadre*. The two godparents, who may never have met each other before the ceremony, become *compadres*. The system, called *compadrazco*, is Catholic Spanish in origin; the word *compadre* in Spanish means godfather.

The Filipino kinship system adopted the religious ritual more as a means to enlarge the group through ritual kinship than for religious reasons. Sponsors at religious rituals in the Philippines have escalated in number and six or eight godparents are common. Prestigious members of the community, such as public officials, are popular choices for godparents. (The *compadre* system extends to weddings and confirmations. Sponsors for these events are also godparents, and the *compadre* bond applies to parents and co-sponsors.) To stand as godfather at a baptism has now become a quasi-official role; most big public officials have godchildren numbering in the hundreds if not thousands. A measure of the importance of a wedding or baptism is the prominence of the godparents.

The word *compadre* is charged with ritual kinship links. Doubtless, in pre-hispanic days, the kinship group expanded through rituals such as the blood compact described by various Spanish chroniclers of the period. The blood compact required the ritual spilling of some blood mixed with wine and drunk by two parties who then become blood brothers. The Christianized *compadre* ritual is regarded more seriously in smaller towns steeped in tradition, whereas in larger population centres the *compadre* bonds are treated more casually. The popular address, *pare*, a vulgarization of *compadre*, is now applied loosely even to total strangers.

## Baptism: Foreigners' Guide

Westerners enjoy a high regard in the Philippines, as most occupy positions of some importance, so they are often asked to act as sponsors to baptisms and weddings. Since it is deemed an honour to be asked, it is not easy to turn down such a request without causing *hiya*; it is best to accept. In any case, it is not expected that a

49

*A baptismal ceremony. The child is a girl so the godmother holds her while the parents, godfather, other sponsors and relatives look on.*

Westerner understands fully the obligations of godfatherhood. Provided you do not demonstrate involvement in the intricacies of the kinship group, your ceremonial role will be considered honour enough.

A sponsor at baptism carries the child during the brief ceremony. Both the godfather and the godmother enjoy equal importance. By custom if the child is a male the godfather is considered more important, if female, the godmother. Traditionally only one sponsor, a godmother, was selected if the child was a girl, a godfather if the child was male, but the popularity of the *compadre* system has now made it common for each child to have both godfather and godmother; at times five sets of sponsors or more. In these cases, the godparents enjoy equal importance, although the sex of the child would place greater importance on the sponsor of similar gender.

Needless to say, you are expected to be dressed smartly as befits the occasion: it is an important ceremony for the parents of the child.

As godparent, it is courteous to offer to pay for the church rites;

while not expensive, fees vary depending on the elaborateness of rites (whether it is at the side altar or the front altar, whether bells are rung, etc.). Also it is proper to give the godchild a gift, its measure depending on one's generosity. Among the upper middle class and the wealthy a popular gift is a silver cup or spoon-and-fork set for the baby, a pair of gold earrings for a female godchild, or a set of embroidered baby clothes. Something practical but nice for the baby is a safe rule. The parents put up a feast which could be elaborate (with a horde of guests), or modest (confined to a small circle), with the godparents as guests of honour.

Finally, following tradition, some godparents scatter a 'shower' of small change as a wish for prosperity for the godchild. Obviously, it is a good idea to bring with you a small packet of coins, say twenty pesos' worth of ten centavo coins, as a token shower. A grandiose *sabog* (as the shower of coins is called) would be several hundred pesos in fifty centavo and one peso coins (or even larger bills). Usually only children and teenaged girls participate actively in grappling for coins; elders who gather coins do so only because they believe it will bring them luck, since *hiya* would make it unseemly for adults to appear grasping and materialistic.

By tradition, obligations of the godparents are lifelong. The godchild's only obligation is to pay them due respect. Material help is not vital, but an effort to help in the form of obtaining jobs, writing letters of recommendation and references are expected; which explains why public officials who are obviously in a position to offer patronage are sought-after godparents.

## Baptism Etiquette

1. Participants meet at the church and fill out the registration forms.
2. The *ninong* or godfather is expected to pay for the services. Services vary according to how elaborate you want the ritual to be. Payment is made during the registration.

3. Participants enter the church and the priest performs the ceremony. The sponsor holds the child. If the child is a girl, the godmother holds it; if it is a boy, the godfather carries the child.
4. After the ceremony the party proceeds to a feast hosted by the parents. In a ceremony involving prominent people, the sponsors throw a shower of coins to the assembled guests. Children are given full play in scrambling for coins while adults show only a token participation, picking up a few coins for good luck, and often giving these to the children.
5. Dress is semi-formal (party attire).

## *Filipino Wedding*

Sponsors at weddings hold the places of honour. In the social climbing game, the more important the sponsor the greater the prestige for the two families joined in kinship at a wedding. Naturally the ultimate sponsor would have to be the President of the Philippines, and then on down the social ladder to cabinet secretaries and prominent personalities. Unlike the baptismal godparent, the wedding godparent acquires overnight two adult godchildren practically ready to assume more responsible tasks in society; therefore the obligation to assist in providing career opportunities to the godchild is more immediate. For the ceremony itself, however, all that is expected from a godparent is a wedding gift commensurate with the role of sponsor.

Wedding rites are generally church ceremonies. Elaborate weddings can evolve not only multiple sponsors, but an entourage of flower girls, a ringbearer (both roles performed by children), bridesmaids, maid-of-honour, candle-sponsors, cord-sponsors, and veil-sponsors, aside from main, godparent sponsors.

By Philippine standards, weddings move fairly promptly with only the bride allowed a leeway for tardiness. (A bride must not seem too eager by appearing too early at her wedding.) Only a very important sponsor can get away with being later than the bride.

Unlike invitations to a feast when people do not like to appear too anxious to eat and so deliberately come late, there is no *hiya* in being early to a wedding.

## *Wedding Sponsor*

The sponsors stand at the altar front with the married couple kneeling during the usual time at Mass. At the end of the ceremonies, sponsors sign the wedding papers as witnesses. At this point you as sponsor should be ready because the sacristan or some church helper will appear with a plate and sponsors are expected to make a small donation. If you are not prepared, you may find yourself staring at the plate with nothing to give; or, having no small bills to offer, it will cost you the only very large bill in your wallet.

You may be asked to act not as the main godfather sponsor, but as candle, veil or cord-sponsor, roles given to friends of the bride or groom. The candle-sponsor lights the candle at the altar and puts this out before the end of the ceremony. If you are a candle-sponsor,

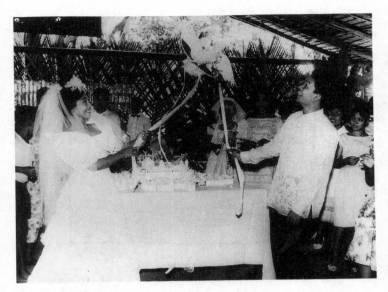

*Releasing a pair of doves, a ritual performed during the wedding reception.*

bring a cigarette lighter that works. The veil-sponsor places a veil over both bride and groom, and the cord-sponsor, a cord. Veil and cord are supplied by the wedding party, and usually someone will signal the sponsors when to perform their part. These sponsors come in pairs, a male and a female for each ritual.

## Wedding Feast

A banquet is held after the wedding, in some public restaurant or social club. Honoured guests are given a place at the head table with the bride and groom, their parents, and the wedding entourage. Sometimes a bell-shaped white paper cage hangs in a conspicuous place near the head table and the bride and groom pull long, white, silken ribbons attached to the cage, releasing white pigeons or doves that create a minor havoc among the tables of guests until caught.

*A traditional barrio wedding where peso bills are pinned to the clothes of the bride and groom, gifts to start them off in life.*

The bride and groom assist each other in cutting the wedding cake, at times made by some relative noted for culinary skills and artistry as her wedding contribution; but just as often the cake is a part of a catered affair. The couple may exchange mouthfuls of cake. Unmarried female guests approach the head table and pick up little trinkets tied with ribbons in the wedding cake, which have their marital fortunes inscribed as in a fortune cookie. Small boxes of the cake, with the initials of the bride and groom, are distributed to the guests as mementos (bringing home food from a feast is a Filipino custom). Toasts and speeches are now fashionable. A card of thanks acknowledging your gift is written by the new bride a month or two later, when the couple have settled down.

Many features of the wedding, including the Catholic church ceremony, are Western adaptations. In ritual form, weddings follow Spanish tradition, but the addition of the best man and bridesmaids, and sometimes ushers, are borrowed from American wedding practice. As long as it means addition, the kinship group will be happy to make new features part of the ceremony. As a well-known political figure, the late 'Amang' Rodriguez (former Senate President and head of the Nationalist Party) observed: 'Politics is addition.'

If you are invited to a Filipino wedding you may attend both church ceremony and wedding banquet; a few miss the church ritual and proceed directly to the feast. As in all Filipino social affairs, fine clothes are the rule.

After the religious rites the bride and groom leave the church for the banquet hall and stand at the entrance to receive guests. One congratulates the groom, but it is not good form to congratulate the bride—she gets your good wishes. Filipinas are demure, and the male is deemed to have conquered and won fair lady.

Usually near the entrance is a table where all the wedding gifts are placed. After the banquet, guests bid farewell and reiterate good wishes to the couple. Customs in rural areas vary by region. In some traditional *barrio* weddings, peso bills are pinned to the clothes of the bride and groom, practical gifts to start them off in married life.

## WEDDING ETIQUETTE

### Pre-Nuptial Parties

The bride-to-be is given one or more nuptial parties by her relatives and friends. She may be given a kitchen, bathroom or bedroom shower, which are informal hen parties.

1. The kitchen shower is the most common type of pre-nuptial party. Guests bring presents that are used in the kitchen.
2. Appropriate presents for the bathroom shower are towels, soap, soap dishes and other bathroom accessories.

3. Presents for a bedroom shower are bedsheets, pillowcases, nighties, etc.

## Wedding Gifts

Customary gifts are silverware, crystal, vases, wine-glasses and other household items. You can send your gift ahead to either the bride's or the groom's house, whichever of the two invited you.

## The Nuptial Mass

All guests are invited to the nuptial Mass as well as to the reception, and most attend both. After the nuptial rites, as the bride and groom walk out of the church, they are showered with rice. This is believed to bring them prosperity. They then proceed to the reception and the guests follow.

## The Reception

1. The reception may be held at a big restaurant, at the house of the bride's or the groom's parents, or at a private club like the Club Filipino or the Polo Club.
2. The bride and groom stand at the entrance and greet the guests as they come in. There is a table on one side where the gifts are placed by those who choose to bring their gift to the reception.
3. The reception is either breakfast or dinner. For the more well-to-do, it is usually dinner.
4. After the meal, the bride and groom cut the cake and feed each other a spoonful of it. After this, all the unmarried girl guests go and pull a ribbon from the cake, at the end of which is attached a charm containing a piece of paper with a saying on it, like those found in fortune cookies.
5. The bride and groom pull the cord of a bell hanging from the ceiling which releases two doves. This is the final ritual. The couple, together with the bridal entourage, then go to a photographer's studio for a photography session.

## *Wedding Anniversaries*

The wedding anniversaries usually celebrated are the Silver Anniversary (25 years), the Ruby Anniversary (40 years) and the Golden Anniversary (50 years). These anniversaries are celebrated with big parties. In some cases the couple renew their vows and re-enact their wedding with their children and grandchildren as bridesmaids and flower girls.

It is customary to give a present which is in accordance with the anniversary motif (e.g. silver for the 25th, something red for the Ruby, gold or something with a gold design for the 50th).

## *Relatives are Important, but ...*

The *compadre* system borrowed from Christian rituals assures growth for the extended family system, and also allows flexible development of a kinship group outside the socially and economically incestuous prison of blood relatives. A migrant from some small town can become part of a kinship group in Manila through the *compadre* system. While individuals rely on immediate relatives for support and mutual benefit, they do not hesitate to enter into social relationships with non-kin, who may be physically more accessible or able to offer better professional service or economic benefits. The kinship group is therefore partially an association within a family kin group and partially of the individual's making.

An individual is not just a passive unit of the family group he is born into; he redefines and reshapes his kinship universe by marriage and also by personal selection, entering into ritual *compadre* relationships with individuals and kinship groups of his choice. As Fr. Frank Lynch observed about kinship groups: 'Relatives are important but the importance is relative.'

## *Guide to the Kinship System*

You do not have to fully understand the intricate interweaving of kinship groups in the Philippine society: many Filipinos have not given it much conscious thought either. What is important is to recognize its existence, and to apply this perspective when functioning in the Philippine society. For instance, what may be perceived as outright nepotism in family corporations or even government institutions may be regarded as an accommodation to the kinship system. Only when related to outright disaster, incompetence and corruption, does this nepotism become a grievous sin to Filipinos.

A Filipino official is torn between his official duties and his kinship obligations. This contradiction and duality is a mark of Philippine contemporary society. A policeman is obviously remiss in his duty if he does not turn in a culprit who happens to be his son, but the kinship group would surely regard him as remiss as a father if he does not use his powers to shield his son who happens to be a culprit. A policeman would never issue a traffic ticket to his god-father the public official, for how could a godchild who owes his job to his *ninong* show such ingratitude?

This dilemma is reported by Arce and Poblador in a study on *Formal Organizations in the Philippines. Motivation, Behaviour, Structure and Change*: 'There seems to be a consensus that the company rule barring the employment of an individual who is already related to someone in the company is a good thing. Theo-retically, even fictive kinship (*kumpare*) is included in the prohibi-tion. Among the workers, however, contracting fictive relationships with one another is much sought after. The managers frown on the practice but admit that there is not much that they can do to curb it.'

The kinship structure, furthermore, places group pressure not only on the individual but on those who may threaten the group by harming a member. In *Understanding Filipino Values*, Andres points out that 'Each person is an outward extension of his family and kin group. If a worker is caught stealing, it is said, "*Ang pamilya niya' y mahihiya sa lipunan*" (his family is shamed before society). The "shame" of the worker is the "shame" of the family and kin group. Even when an individual has ignored a "shaming" remark or situation, his family may take up the issue for the family position is involved. Criticism of a person is not as an individual *qua* individual, but as a representative of a family and kin group. There are cases in which incompetent school-teachers were not fired because such an action would make both the dismissed person and his relatives *kahiya-hiya*. The supervisors themselves fear that the relatives of the dismissed person may do them actual physical harm, in addition to the inevitable threats and reprimands for the supervisors' harsh and terrible treatment.'

Philippine society is a universe of kinship groups, each putting group pressure into play. What is improper for the rest of society is expected to be overlooked when it involves a member of the kinship group because to do otherwise is to embarrass the group who loses self-control once their *amor-propio* is damaged. Rivalry between kinship groups is the hallmark of Philippine society and politics. It has been observed that even among Filipino communities living abroad, there are invariably two or more rival organizations. The foreign visitor who may think he has finally become considered part of a group may suddenly find he has also gained the animosity of a rival group.

It is important not to be too involved and committed to one given group, if one is to function in a larger social scheme. The person who manages to maintain the goodwill of as many groups as possible is master of the Philippine situation; the only other alternative is to belong to the biggest and most powerful kinship group with links to the nationwide power structure. A recent study by John F. Doherrty, S.J. entitled, *Who Controls the Economy: Some Need Not Try As Hard As Others*, claims that in the whole country only 81 individuals control 453 major corporations all interlocked with one another with government sanction. This should give some insight into the dynamics of power of the kinship group carried to its very peak.

# Chapter Four

# FIESTA: KINSHIP GROUP CONVENTION

There is a Philippine fiesta going on somewhere in the archipelago practically throughout the year. Some town fiestas are famous nationwide: the Ati-atihan in Kalibo, Aklan, the Pahiyas of Lucban, Quezon, the fluvial fiesta of Bocaue, Bulacan, the Christmas Eve lantern festival in San Fernando Pampanga, the Carabao festival in Gapan, and the feast of the Black Nazarene in Quiapo, Manila, to name a few. Town fiestas are usually celebrated during the feast of the patron saint of the town. In the dim past, some of these fiestas were probably ancient rites associated with prayers for rain and good harvest or for the rivers and seas to yield bountiful fish. Among the Tagbanwa, a cultural minority group from the island of Palawan, three-day festivities are held during the clearing of a forest area for planting.

Early Catholic missionaries harnessed some of these community practices towards religious ends by introducing Catholic reasons and rites. On the other hand water-dousing events in fiestas today appear to be linked to Buddhist rites in the past similar to the celebrated Songkran (Thai New Year) celebrations in Thailand's Chiang Mai.

Everyone is welcome at a fiesta. There could be one in your neighbourhood in the city. A fiesta revolves around the parish church, and could be limited to only a city district (such as the fiesta in Quiapo), just one *barrio*, or it could embrace the whole town. It is usual for a fiesta to last three days. At fiesta time the entire community participates; in Kalibo's Ati-atihan, all the townspeople, from the Mayor to the street beggar, spill out into the streets in the thousands to dance in a procession honouring the Holy Child. The tables of practically every house are laden with food and there are all sorts of public entertainment and activities.

Hospitality is the great theme of all fiestas, so a non-Filipino need not concern himself too much about proper behaviour; there are no strict rules of comportment. Since most fiestas have a religious origin, the church and the patron saint are important symbols, and proper respect is called for when inside a church, or when the image of the patron saint is carried through the streets in a procession.

## Facets of the Fiesta

A town fiesta builds up several days before. There is usually a novena nine days before the town saint's feast day. People work to make their homes as presentable as possible, with fresh paint, new curtains, or simply well scrubbed and polished floors and windows. The streets are decorated with bamboo arches and brightly-coloured paper buntings. The town plaza is made spic-and-span, and a dance is usually held the night of the fiesta. Entertainment in the form of amusement booths, and sidewalk stalls selling trinkets, toys and food add noise and colour. Carousels, ferris wheels and sideshows occupy a section of the plaza near the church.

Fiesta is homecoming for all those studying or working away from their hometowns, and of course these returning sons and daughters bring friends with them. Everyone in town has laboured to prepare food; the pig that has been fattened all year is made ready for the table. Roast pig (*lechon*), is as important a fiesta food as turkey on Thanksgiving Day for Americans, or ham at Christmas for Europeans. Some foods were exclusively fiesta fare in earlier times, like carabao milk fudge (*pastillas*), wrapped in special colou red Japanese tissue paper with intricate handcut designs displaying fiesta motifs or messages, and served to guests at the fiesta of San Miguel, Bulacan. The social importance of food to Filipinos is evident at fiesta time.

American historian John Leddy Phelan claims that the Spaniards had instituted the fiesta in Philippine towns in order to draw the people (who at the time lived in scattered kin group clusters) into one central area, creating a forum for Christianizing the populace. In support of this viewpoint is the colourful and elaborate pageantry associated with the fiesta, which takes varied forms.

In a seaside or riverside town the religious procession which highlights the fiesta will very likely be a fluvial one, with the image carried in a bamboo structure, called *pagoda*, atop a barge. In Angono, Rizal, the fluvial procession is followed by a land procession through the main streets of the town with a lot of water-dousing among participants and onlookers as well. The procession in land-locked towns on the other hand usually starts from the church and winds through the main streets in a circular route that leads back to the church. People carrying candles accompany the image of the patron saint which stands on *carroza*, a special pedestal on wheels.

In Sariaya, Quezon, as soon as the image of the patron saint passes by, children scamper for cookies and other goodies hung on bamboo poles along the street. In Pakil, Laguna, the men and womenfolk perform a curious dance called *turrumba* as they march in procession. In towns where San Isidro Labrador, the patron saint of farmers, is venerated, processions may be composed of gaily decorated bullcarts or, as in Pulilan, Bulacan, of hundreds of massed carabaos decked with flowers.

Another traditional fiesta entertainment was a folk play called *moro-moro* or *comedia*, which acted out in poetry and music mythical tales of kings and princesses, and the conflict between Christians and Moors, an ancient theme from Spanish history. Nowadays, this theatrical form is rarely seen except in small towns with a strong tradition; and in its place one is regaled by amateur singers, or a variety show featuring prominent cinema and television personalities.

To be invited to the home of a prominent member of the town at fiesta time is a signal honour. First a ball is organized by the prominent families of the community. This is an occasion for celebrants to be dressed to the nines. By tradition, the *rigodon* dance which opens the ball calls for the participation of the most important members of the community. In this social happening the less privileged folk are mere spectators, watching outside the enclosed area, the contrast between the two socio-economic classes of Philippine society clearly underscored. Tickets to the ball are sold either to finance the ball itself, for some other activity of the town fiesta, or to support a civil undertaking.

This brief description of the fiesta is to whet your appetite to experience one. There are various spectacular and important ones in different parts of the country. Included in some of these rituals are Lenten rites which are not 'celebrations' but pageants commemorating Christ's crucifixion, a Christian period of mourning. Nevertheless, Filipinos being a gregarious lot, even these events end up with much food and camaraderie turning them into a fiesta.

## *BRIEF GUIDE TO FIESTAS*

Fiestas in Manila are not like those in other parts of the country partly because of the lack of total community spirit in depersonalized Manila. The *comedia* can be seen in Parañaque, outside Manila; you can get information through the Parañaque municipality, the Cultural Center of the Philippines, or the Department of Tourism.

Angono, in Manila's environs, has a fluvial fiesta in honour of San Clemente, in late January. Situated along Laguna Lake, the fluvial procession is joyful; fishermen's canoes scoot around the main barge; wine is passed around among those in the main barge where the image is carried. You are bound to get wet during the fluvial part of the fiesta; if not, the land revellers will, in friendly spirit, douse you with lake water. Angono is the hometown of the celebrated national artist, the late Carlos V. Francisco. His famous paintings often depict this Angono fiesta.

*A fluvial fiesta. A main barge, called* pagoda, *is built to house the image of the town patron saint for the occasion and merrymaking is conducted on the water.*

Near by, in Pateros, during the feast of Santa Marta, the fluvial procession features people dancing atop a tin-topped crocodile pulled by boats along the water hyacinth-clogged river. Pateros is famous for its *balut* duck's eggs.

In Lucban, and in nearby Sariaya, both in Quezon Province, the feast of San Isidro Labrador on May 15 is celebrated with a *pahiyas*; the patron saint of farmers is given special offerings (*pahiyas*) in the form of imaginative displays of agricultural produce as decor. Houses along streets are lined with stalks of rice (*palay*), vegetables and fruits, as well as other material from nature including carabao skulls, dried fish, woven palm hats and fans, and a specially made leaf-shaped rice-flour wafer, called *kiping,* clustered like giant translucent petals in various tints of pink, yellow and green. Many ancestral homes grace Lucban and Sariaya, placing these two fiestas in truly picturesque settings.

Pahiyas *of fruits and other agricultural products honour the patron saint of farmers, San Isidro Labrador.*

*Devotees cover their bodies with soot and prance about the streets in wild abandon during the Ati-ati festival.*

## Ati-atihan

The Ati-atihan in Kalibo has now become much too commercialized. Its spontaneous pleasure has been suffocated by the sheer number of people in the streets. Three decades ago various groups would dance tirelessly as the procession wound several times around the plaza; nowadays you can barely move in the packed mass of revellers while watching out for pickpockets and drunken ruffians.

However, less than an hour's drive out of Kalibo is the tiny town of Ibajay, and here a truer, if smaller, Ati-ati festival can be witnessed. Participants or devotees paint their faces and arms with soot, deck their hair with leaves, and brandish poles topped with strange objects—food offerings, live birds or lizards tied to the poles, and so on. The image of the Holy Child is brought out of the church and carried around the small plaza, while the devotees dance and shout

'Viva Santo Niño' to the pounding of drums. Men dressed in the theatrical *moro-moro* costumes of Christians and Moors, marching with stylized gestures, also escort the image. If you cannot get to Ibajay, the Kalibo fiesta is a mardi-gras affair you can enjoy, making allowances for its commercialized degeneration.

The Ati-atihan is popularly believed to have pre-hispanic origins—celebration of a peace treaty between the early negrito (*ati*) settlers and the Malay immigrants. The wild abandon in the streets, its riotous gaiety, certainly do not conform to the expected solemn religious festival for the Holy Child. The mayor of the town remarked to us some years ago, during our first Ati-atihan visit, 'Here in Kalibo there are no hospitals for the mentally ill because once a year we can all go out into the streets and let go.'

## Lenten Rituals

Lent is a solemn time for Catholics, and Spanish missionaries introduced rites such as flagellation and re-enactments of the climactic tragedy of the life of Jesus—the washing of the apostles' feet, the way of the cross, the seven last words, and Palm Sunday rites. There are many solemn processions during Holy Week, their importance measured by the number of religious images on *carrozas* participating. Witnessing Lenten rites gives one a good insight into Philippine society.

Short theatrical folk plays or *sinakulo* present biblical stories as well as passages from the life of Christ, one favourite being the episode of Judas and the thirty pieces of silver. The players are selected from the community, and obviously in selecting the roles for Jesus and Mary much more than thespian abilities come into play. Prominent cinema personalities are sometimes invited to play the lead roles.

Lenten rites have also been adopted in non-Christian folk rituals, borrowing the exotic features of the elaborate Spanish Catholic ceremonies to perpetuate occult beliefs. A popular belief is that one

*A penitent in a Lenten procession carrying a cross.*

*An early evening procession is the hallmark of every town fiesta or important religious event. Ladies wear veils and all devotees carry lighted candles. The image is taken around the main streets before being returned to the church.*

may obtain supernatural strength on the night of Good Friday by performing certain rituals, such as standing under the clustered flowers of the banana plant in expectation of a talisman that could magically drop into one's mouth at midnight, or by testing amulets in the deep forests of the occult mountain, Mount Banahaw.

As Lenten rites demonstrate, folk Catholicism among Filipinos runs the gamut of orthodox Christian beliefs and 'pagan' occult practices. It reveals folk imagination, a deep persistence of pre-Christian values, and the ability to selectively borrow outward motifs of Christian religion for their own set of beliefs and values.

Folk Catholicism is a characteristic of Filipino society vital to the understanding of the Filipino character. For centuries vocal members of the clergy have lamented that many Filipinos, especially in rural areas where the majority live, go to church only three times in their lives—when they are christened, when they marry, and when their corpses receive last rites; an exaggerated charge, because Filipinos also go to church to attend their kin's and friends' baptisms, weddings, and funerals, and Mass at Christmas and fiesta time. It is true not many bother to go to church outside of these social occasions.

## Moriones: *Masked Devotees*

Marinduque island, just off Batangas Province in Luzon, commemorates Lent with a strong dose of folk Catholicism. Marinduque in Lent is worth a visit for insights into Filipino folkways. Throughout Holy Week, three towns—Mogpog, Gasan, and Boac—become an open total theatre for townsmen wearing wooden masks topped by paper helmets and flowers. The devotees are dressed as Roman soldiers of Christ's era. The *moriones* mill about the town, some 'clacking' two musical sticks of wood together. They attend the nightly processions.

On Easter Sunday, one of these masked figures, who portrays Longino the soldier, said to have stabbed Christ with a spear, runs about the town to proclaim that Christ has risen. According to popular myth, Longino is a Roman centurion, blind in one eye, who is miraculously healed by Christ's blood spilling on his blind eye when he jabs the crucified figure. He is assigned to watch the tomb of the dead Jesus where he witnesses the resurrection, and as he gives testimony to the Risen Christ he is killed by fellow Roman soldiers. In legend he is the first Christian martyr.

The Marinduque Longino is chased about the town by the other *moriones* and is captured three times, escaping twice; on his third capture, as he proclaims to the spectators what he has witnessed, a *morion* strikes him down with a sword in a mock beheading. *Moriones* carry his 'body' through town into church, ending the ceremonies. These days the mock chase and beheading are held in an enclosed area with viewing stands provided for spectators as the ceremonies have become so popular.

*Morion* masks are carved out of wood, the faces painted a garish red with a large nose and huge staring eyes, forming a curious graphic image of how the Filipino folk see Romans, or in fact Westerners in general: red-faced, big-nosed, gaping mouths, with mean or imbecilic expressions. Folk imagination extends beyond Roman imagery into science fiction, with one-eyed or triple-faced masks inspired by Hollywood films; *Star Wars* and *ET* have their counterparts among some masked participants. Vegetal material is also used for masks: coconuts, feathers, plant fibres, baskets, seashells, sago-sago seeds.

## Other Lenten Rites

Also on Easter Sunday, in many towns in the Philippines, the Lenten ceremony called 'Salubong' is performed. Statues of the Blessed Virgin (wearing a black shroud of mourning) and that of the Risen Christ are carried in procession in opposite directions, to meet later under a bamboo arch erected for the occasion.

A young couple, the male dressed in white, the woman in pink, perform a dance with two flags, said to symbolize a life and death struggle and Christ's triumph over death. A little girl dressed as an angel sitting in a box suspended from the top of the bamboo arch, is lowered by means of a pulley. Singing a song announcing Christ has risen, she lifts the veil covering the image of the Blessed Virgin.

## *Importance of a Vow*

During Lenten rites, women cover their heads with leaves, wear purple or black robes, and walk barefoot. Men, stripped to the waist, flagellate themselves with pieces of bamboo tied to a string. Small incisions made on the skin cause slight bleeding and these wounds are whipped rhythmically with the bamboo bits tied to the string—hardly a pleasant practice, in fact discouraged by orthodox Christians, especially the modern-minded clergy.

These rituals are *panata*, vows or oaths contracting oneself to participate in the ritual in acknowledgement of some favour granted, some wish fulfilled, by the saint or deity one venerates. The *panata* is nothing more than a carry-over of the Filipino *utang na loob* mechanics, although it must be said that performance in rituals as a contract with gods is also Hindu (witness the *kavadi* carriers at Thaipusam, or firewalkers at Theemithi) and Christian (Masses attended or paid for, novenas for a special request).

Someone ill may seek health, promising to participate if healed; another may pass an exam prayed for, still another prays for children. Participation in the religious portion of fiestas (including cash donations) is often a matter of panata.

It was a common practice for wealthy landlords to donate the harvest or income from a portion of land to the patron saint. The *de facto* ownership by the patron saint over the property's income was respected by the landowner's kin; to dispose of such land would be deemed practically sacrilegious. Many wealthy patrons owned their own larger than life-sized religious statuary of a family patron saint, complete with *carroza*, which participated in the religious processions at fiesta time.

## Christmas Festivals

Christmas is also a period of celebration and pageantry. In Valenzuela, Bulacan, the search for a room by Mary and Joseph during their visit to Bethlehem is re-enacted by a couple who visit assignated houses asking, in song, for a room; each time of course they are rebuffed in the form of poetry by the house owner until the they reach the town plaza where a *belen* (an effigy of the Christmas nativity) stands. Singing of the birth of the Holy Child, the couple as Mary and Joseph pick up the figure of the child Jesus from the manger, and carry it inside the church at the stroke of midnight for Christmas Mass.

Also on Christmas Eve, in San Fernando Pampanga, there is a spectacular lantern festival. The Christmas lantern is the Filipino Christmas motif. It represents the star of Bethlehem, signifying not only the birth of Christ, but also the guiding light for the Three Wise Men, the spirit of hospitality. Most Filipino children have, sometime in their lives, made a Christmas lantern, usually of bamboo strips and coloured Japanese tissue paper. The wealthiest of mansions and the poorest of shanties express their Christmas spirit by hanging a Christmas lantern over a house window.

The San Fernando lanterns are the ultimate development of this tradition because these are more than ten feet in diameter, mounted on the front of trucks. Intricate designs are created by applying different layers of coloured translucent tissue paper, producing various tones of each colour. The lanterns are electronically lighted by hundreds of lights flashing on and off or 'moving' in a programmed series. An electric generator at the back of the truck applies the power, while the lighting patterns and designs are manipulated through countless switches and wires by hand or a rotating drum. Each lantern is accompanied by a musical band which plays to the beat of the flashing lights.

Small replicas of the lantern, minus the complex lighting, are carried by the *barrio* folk associated with that particular lantern.

Various *barrios* of San Fernando create their own giant lanterns and gather at the town plaza on Christmas Eve where the most beautiful lantern is selected by a panel. Thousands of people jam the plaza to witness the competition and event. The lanterns are made at great expense; *barrio* and kin-group honour is at stake.

Because December and January are in the harvest season, fiestas during this period are generally bountiful. Other fiestas of the season are the feast of the Three Kings on 6 January, the Angono fiesta (San Clemente), the Ati-atihan in Kalibo and Ibajay, and the Dinagyang in Iloilo.

## *Christmas Season Etiquette*

1. Christmas is the time to show appreciation to maids, garbage collectors, drivers, gardeners, washerwomen, security guards.
2. *Utang na loob* is in full play. It is an opportunity to acknowledge a debt through a token gift. Doctors especially are showered with gifts at Christmastime.
3. Food always makes a good gift and is much appreciated, especially if it is a specialty.
4. A favourite custom among young people in Manila (university students and even among office mates) is a game called 'Chris Kindle' or 'Mama Kindle' where gifts are exchanged.
5. Godchildren expect gifts from their *ninongs*. In turn, they pay their godparents a courtesy call, but this is not strictly enforced nowadays.
6. Children visit parents and grandparents on Christmas Day, usually spending it together as a family.

## *Maytime Fiestas*

Most of the fiestas, however, occur at Maytime. It is the last month of the dry season, just before the rains and the planting season, the farmer's leisure month and thus the perfect fiesta hour. Feasts of patron saints that fall during awkward times are often postponed to

May. In the Tagalog region alone, Frank Lynch counted 52 town fiestas in May. Fiestas also being a prayer for rain and an invocation to the gods for a good harvest and a bountiful supply of fish, May is the propitious month. May weather is generally cooperative for outdoor ceremonies. Rain inevitably follows the fiestas.

Santakruzan and Flores de Mayo are social events held in the merry month of May. For these two practices, young girls designated *reinas* (queens), dressed in lavish white gowns, are crowned with a flower tiara. These village beauties parade through the streets in a quasi-religious ceremony. The Santakruzan depicts Queen Helena and the search for the Holy Cross. However, in both this and the Flores de Mayo, the social purpose is to give public tribute to female pulchritude and grace, of girls from childhood to marriageable age.

*A* sagala *and her escort in a Flores de Mayo procession.*

## *Fiesta Games*

Town fiestas give importance to social, non-religious events. Apart from feasting, public entertainment is set up just for the fiesta.

*Palo sebo* and the *juego de anillo* are traditional fiesta games. In *palo sebo*, prize money in a bag atop a greased bamboo pole belongs to the daring, agile boy or young man who can get to the slippery top. The *juego de anillo* is a ring game introduced by the Spaniards; the aim is to pierce suspended rings with a pole; the traditional version is performed by a girl and boy riding a carriage; now boys ride bicycles. Basketball and volleyball competitions are part of a fiesta; also singing, dancing and oratorical contests.

Christenings, confirmations and marriages are timed for the fiesta, a practice linked to a time when priests could service rural parishes only irregularly. Lumping rites at fiesta time when priests, perhaps even a bishop, would be present proved practical.

*Hands to ankle, scaling the pole in the* palo sebo, *to reach the prize money at the very top of the greased pole.*

*The pabitin is a popular feature of many fiestas, especially in the Flores de Mayo. Childhood memories always dredge up the excitement of children reaching for a basket of goodies.*

## The Cockfight

Wallace Stegner, an American writer, wrote: 'You don't know Filipinos until you have seen some little fellow who has trained a chicken for months put it into the ring against another's rooster. He bets everything he owns on it, steals his wife's savings, sells his children's shirts to raise a peso. If he wins, glorious; if in one pass his rooster gets its throat cut, then you will see how a philosopher takes disaster ...' A cockfight is another major fiesta feature.

Cockfighting was around when the first Spaniard visited Palawan island, but the creation of urban areas by the Spaniards and the establishment of fiesta made cockfighting an institution. In any rural area one sees some man squatting in the shade, massaging, blowing smoke, and grooming his fighting rooster. Wags observed that in a fire a Filipino will rescue his fighting cock before his family or possessions. True to form, well-known poet and cocker, Manuel Bernabe, lost house, medals and certificates of honour as bard of Parañaque, in a fire—but salvaged all his roosters.

Most large towns have a cockpit, a circular structure with a central pit or arena, and colosseum-style wooden bleachers. A roof keeps out sun and rain, while the absence of walls (the skeletal structure of the stands serves as the enclosure) permits light and ventilation. A rooster in hand serves as a pass, otherwise an admission fee is charged.

Having trained their roosters for months, cockers negotiate among themselves for a suitable match. Razor-sharp spurs attached, roosters are placed in the arena, and the betting begins. When roosters are of the same colour, one handler wears a hat, and bets are made on the one 'with a hat' or the one 'without'. Prominent cockers sit at ringside. The bookmaker (*casador*) takes the bets. If there is much more money for one rooster than the other, he distributes some bets among the prominent cockers, calling them by name and the amounts they will answer for; usually these cockers nod in agreement. The *casador* has a remarkable memory for faces, bets taken in a split second of hand gestures and calls, and the changing odds given during a match. Reneging on a bet is inadvisable. The cockfight is over in minutes, and 'doctors' perform skilled surgery on wounds. The loser takes his dead rooster home and cooks it in a special dish called *talunan*, meaning 'loser's repast'.

The cockfight remains popular despite efforts to eradicate it as an unproductive gambling vice, cruel to animals. A cockpit code of behaviour speaks of community honour not as visible in the general society. 'Fixed' fights are not the rule despite heavy betting. Cockfighting is democratic in the sense that the poorest cocker can pit his rooster against the most prominent town official and win, although the introduction of expensive imported breeds has changed the quality of cockfighting. The ready acquiescence of prominent cockers to the *casador* committing them to bets just to get the fight going shows strong communal spirit and trust. Cockfighting in the Philippines reveals a social institution with standards which, in contrast to the national scene, appear high and workable.

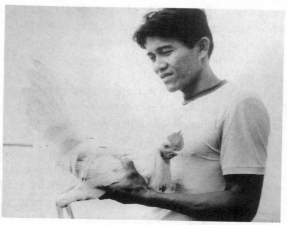

*A man and his fighting rooster are close companions.*

79

## *What Fiestas Are All About*

Many things Filipino come together at the fiesta. Commercial enterprises mushroom temporarily. Itinerant groups move about from fiesta to fiesta—vendors, entertainers, hairdressers, medicine-men, pickpockets, beggars. Naturally politicians seize the fiesta as an opportune event for winning votes.

It is homecoming for many members who work elsewhere for the rest of the year. Prominent citizens are honoured. It is a time of renewal; houses are repaired and cleaned, streets and public places decorated, religious icons repainted or re-dressed. It is an outlet for folk art and folk creativity.

People are dressed in their best. The town is truly alive. There are the *gigantes*, paper and cloth 'giants'. Inside these light bamboo constructions portraying Gulliver-like people are children who, for a few days, feel ten feet tall. There is the special food, the town's specialities to savour. There are old friends and kin to see. There are the beauty queens and the lovely young ladies with their shy, timid escorts looking uncomfortable in new clothes and shiny shoes.

Crowded stalls, roving bands of musicians, religious proces-sions, and crowded church interiors; cockfights, games and contests; the lavish ball, school exhibits; all these seem to come together naturally and effortlessly. Actually they are the result of a lot of organization and expense.

The mechanics behind each fiesta reveal the dynamics that cause Filipino society to hum. Fiestas are not spontaneous but are carefully discussed, financed, organized, rehearsed, and executed by key townspeople. Plans are worked out well in advance, responsibilities parcelled out and tasks delegated. Individuals and organizations pitch in to donate money or services. Sale of tickets representing votes tor beauty contests, and tickets to social affairs and fashion shows generate funds. Sponsors are given full credit for their contributions, such public acknowledgement being an important part of fiesta activities.

*Two gigantes carousing at the beach with fiesta revellers. These papier-mâché giants are seen in several town fiestas, such as this one at Marinduque.*

Wealthier and more prominent community members provide logistical support to the fiesta as well as organizational skills. The signal honour of being designated *hermano mayor* (passed around among only a handful of individuals in the town) makes it hard to refuse. For the prestige, the *hermano mayor* foots the bill for various fiesta features, from meals for the church choir, to church decorations and the open-house table spread over several days. Without the support of key inhabitants of the town there would be no fiesta. In this way, those who are well off share their largesse with the rest of the community. At times people go into debt to provide something for the feast table since it would be *hiya* to have only a meagre repast. The 'takeaway' custom of sending guests home with extra food from the feast table further accentuates this spirit of sharing.

The Filipino's genius for organization as well as his boundless energy are apparent at fiesta time, yet all the events seem to unravel naturally without a visible organizing machinery. Where the Filipino sense of community is strongest, there the fiesta spirit is brightest.

## Renewing Kinship Ties

The gathering of the clan at fiesta time is also the occasion for renewing kinship ties. Marriages, confirmations and baptisms extend the kinship group by rituals. It is an occasion to reaffirm friendship and allegiance. Poor relations and *compadres* from smaller *barrios* flock to town to visit and offer to serve guests or assist at the kitchens of wealthier relatives or landlords in recognition of their *utang na loob* for past favours or their need for future help.

Fiesta is the day of the kinship group, the period of consolidation and growth for the *barangay*. The religious rites affirm the town's spiritual allegiance and aspirations. As Lynch observed: 'The town has, as it were, an implicit pact with the patron; it is expected that the patron will take care of the community if the townspeople fulfill their obligation to celebrate the saint's day in proper fashion. Some have characterized this attitude as one in which the town "buys protection", but those observers are more inspired to see in this conception of the fiesta a natural application of the principle of reciprocity so common in Filipino social life.'

Fiesta time tells the Filipino where he came from and who he is. The Filipino organism comes alive, fed by rituals and the coming together of the kin.

## Trying to Put Down the Fiesta

In the early 1960s, a distinguished member of the Philippine Senate lamented the lavish, unproductive costs of fiestas, estimating the expense then to be about two hundred million pesos annually. The good Senator sought to harness fiesta expenses and community energy to more productive use, such as agricultural shows. By limiting expenses lavished on the feast table, the savings could build capital formation for community enterprises, he suggested.

The Senator's first problem was that people, particularly in the mass media, falsely accused him of seeking to abolish the fiestas, which of course was not his intention at all. But it was really when he tried to get people to be less lavish and more productive with fiesta spending that he was overwhelmed with the futility of it all.

His eager, young, idealistic corps of crusaders toured the towns speechifying before crowds in town plazas, of necessity seeking the support of influential townsmen to rally the townspeople; these prominent people, in turn, earnestly and enthusiastically greeted the Senator and his crusaders with typical Filipino hospitality, wining and dining their guests the only way they knew how—fiesta style. The movement itself had simply triggered another fiesta, or more accurately, the kin-group dynamics causing fiesta-type spending in support of the movement. The Senator's well-intentioned campaign did not end with a bang or a whimper but rather, as one wag noted, 'with a burp'.

# Chapter Five

# A SURVIVAL KIT

After two years in the Philippines, an American Peace Corps Volunteer wrote one of his colleagues: 'I remember how quickly I discovered that people didn't understand me. The simplest things to me seemed not at all familiar to them. I tried to explain, but the further I got into an explanation, the sillier I looked; suddenly I felt undermined; the most basic premises, values and understandings were of no help to me with the people here when I first faced them, for these understandings and ways of doing and seeing things just didn't exist even. There was a big gap.

'This gap is a crucial thing. What choices do I have when I see that the most basic things I act on and am comforted by are not understood in the least by someone else I am working or living with? When that queasy feeling of groping and groping uselessly, desperately for a bridge, some tie, something which will make us less separate, will make us feel recognized by the other, begins to make me tremble and feel utterly sealed away from the other, what do I do?' (Albert G. Bradford, from *Cultural Confrontation in the Philippines* by David L. Szanton.)

When day-to-day social exchanges fail to meet their expectations, some people become frustrated and antagonistic. These individuals are your cartoon image of the tourists who stand out against the landscape in a curious mixture of informal hometown wear and outlandish souvenir hats and geegaws made for tourists and sold in the hotel lobby shops. As pathetic as it appears, many expatriates live their lives out on foreign soil all over the world pining for the mother country, miserable about conditions around them and thoroughly mystified that the alien culture behaves contrary to their expectations. Many cultivate a patronizing attitude towards the 'natives', developing a protective armour of arrogant superiority.

Nothing can be done for the fossilized psyches; they must have their gin and tonics in their private clubs, bashing the habitat they have themselves chosen to inhabit. They live marching to the beat of a different drummer in a place where there are no drums. They build Little Englands, Little Americas, Little Chinas, light years away from their motherland, hearts and stomachs living elsewhere.

Others respond to culture shock by going to the other extreme: they surrender totally to the cultural environment and go native; in the Philippine situation this would mean actually 'becoming Filipino'. Such an option resolves the cultural conflict at the expense of renouncing or losing one's past. These individuals solve the problems of cultural conflict by then assuming the problems of their adopted society, its tensions, anxieties and contradictions.

For the majority of non-Filipinos living in the Philippines, however, neither alternative is satisfactory. What they seek, in the throes of culture shock, is to communicate clearly and to understand the differences between their culture and Filipino society. Such victims of culture shock are not prepared to atrophy their identity or lose it; they want to expand their consciousness and find themselves.

## CULTURAL FATIGUE

Nevertheless, even after surviving the initial shock and accepting the differences, keeping score between two diverse lifestyles and value systems begins to grate. Despite open-mindedness and enthusiasm for learning about a new cultural environment, cultural fatigue sets in. Writing about the US Peace Corps programme in the Philippines, Szanton in *Cultural Confrontation in the Philippines* notes:

'Cultural fatigue is the physical and emotional exhaustion that almost invariably results from the infinite series of minute adjustments required for long-term survival in an alien culture. Living and working overseas generally requires that one must suspend his automatic evaluations and judgments; that he must supply new interpretations to seemingly familiar behaviour and that he must demand of himself constant alterations in the style and content of his activity. Whether this process is conscious or unconscious, successful or unsuccessful, it consumes an enormous amount of energy, leaving the individual decidedly fatigued ... One interesting thing about the fatigue of many of the PCVs is that it so closely resembled the fatigue observed by Guthrie in the behaviour of American business and government personnel in Manila. Interpersonal behaviour of the traditional Philippine nature tended to be viewed in a negative light. Strong Philippine family ties came to be seen as "clannishness", personal sensitivity as "sulkiness", concern for reciprocity as "scheming", deference to age and status as "obsequiousness", ignoring disagreements and avoiding unpleasant subjects as "dishonesty", and lavish hospitality as "wastefulness".'

Survival of foreigners in the Philippines depends on their knowledge and appreciation of Filipino ways of thought and action while preserving their own cultural identity and sanity. Not easy when you are trying to catch an important meeting and the driver has gone off for a cup of coffee, and rushing back to your office to tell your client you'll be late, to find the telephone has lost its dial tone, and, when you manage to grab a taxi, it crawls (meter not flagged down) in a traffic tangle in pouring rain and flooded streets, to your destination at last—to discover the entire building in darkness and your client gone home because of the 'brownout' (power stoppage) in the area.

Trying to see things the Filipino way soon becomes a real threat to one's identity. Szanton viewed it in this light: 'The typical (Peace Corps) Volunteer cherished directness, sincerity, efficiency, and quality. Yet all these values were challenged by the foreign culture in which he worked, to the point where pursuit of them could be counter-productive. Realizing this, the volunteer was likely to pose for himself some searching questions, such as, "If all I do is play a part, adjusting my behaviour to my hosts, then what will I be contributing to the community?" And, "Should I be, and can I be, actor enough to be false to what I value as right and good?" And, ultimately, dormant identity problems were likely to reappear in the form of the question, "Can I not be myself?"—which inexorably led to the unnerving, "Who am I?" '

## Differences in Perception

There are no easy answers. The very recognition of a different social pattern with a different set of values, establishes precisely the premise that there is no black-and-white, right-and-wrong, universal perception for human social etiquette outside the specific culture.

To go back to the questions raised by Szanton, and further compound the dilemma he raises, a set of conflicting cultural values is not really that easily categorized into simplistic generalizations, although generalizations do throw the differences into focus: many of the avowed values cherished by American Peace Corps Volunteers, of 'sincerity, efficiency and quality', as cited by Szanton, are not totally and necessarily opposed by Filipino culture.

Filipinos also value sincerity, efficiency and quality, but from very different viewpoints. A sincere person to a Filipino is one who fulfills his obligations and is true to what the society perceives as verbal, or better still, written, commitments, not one who 'tells it like it is' regardless of who gets hurt. The difference is in the perception of sincerity. It is certainly not a matter of foreigners being 'sincere' and Filipinos being 'insincere'.

Concessions made to Filipino culture should never be at the cost of contradicting human values. A foreigner's identity crisis does not cut that deep into the bone. What is required is a re-examination of these various human virtues and vices, and an appreciation of the style and form they take in the society. There are indigenous Filipino words for sincerity and insincerity, efficiency and inefficiency, quality and the lack it—sufficient evidence that these concepts and values do not escape their consciousness.

Szanton points out that the PCVs were instructed emphatically with the observation that Filipinos were 'person-oriented' while Americans were 'goal-oriented', that Filipinos were concerned with 'being' while Americans were motivated by 'doing', revealing clearly that the philosophical viewpoints alter perceptions and that cultural conflict lies in this arena and not in a locked battle between irreconcilable moral values. It is the different emphasis given to these values, not absolute opposition to them, that causes conflict.

The key word that provides resolution to what appear as diametrical opposites is *expectations*. A 'sincere' foreigner is not asked to become an 'insincere' Filipino. Both cultures value sincerity but perceive this very differently. It is one's expectation or preconceived idea that clouds one's judgment concerning such values as sincerity, or efficiency, or quality. For example, the Western, short-term, goal-oriented, 'doing' style places 'sincerity' on a literal, factual, no-nonsense priority level; a Filipino's long-term, person-oriented concern for 'being' sublimates outspokenness to absolute necessity.

## Two Faces of Sincerity

It is curious to note that throughout the history of Philippine-American relations the issue of 'sincerity' has been constantly and consistently raised by the Filipinos and not by Americans—from the initial negotiations with Admiral Dewey to discussions concerning human rights issues today. In the historical context of official State negotiations, Filipino sincerity has been interpreted as naivete, while American deception regarded as fair tactics applied in the valid expediencies of national self-interest by Americans.

A reading of Philippine-American history will bear this out, as various reputable historians (Leon Wolff, *Little Brown Brother*, and *History of the Filipino People* by Agoncillo and Alfonso, just to cite two) bring up the issue. Americans do not hesitate to sugar-coat what they value as 'sincerity' in certain perceived cultural situations such as in negotiations with other nations, or in the use of euphemism in public statements by US State officials and politicians, which turn out to be far from sincere. Americans also accept readily the exaggeration of commercial advertising which falls short of the strict demands of the term 'sincerity', but these have been re-interpreted into American cultural expectations. Americans would consider Filipinos foolish to believe at face value US official negotiators who are out to drive a hard bargain, or door-to-door salesmen, and TV advertising.

In this context Filipino cultural expectations are misled, and Filipinos are 'taken in'. Americans automatically adjust expectations of sincerity when dealing with used car salesmen, politicians, and official press releases. Filipinos not familiar with this cultural context of sincerity receive false signals and succumb much too readily to hardsell advertising. One example is the way impoverished Filipina mothers buy powdered or canned milk at great expense, having been deluded by American advertising into thinking this is better, healthier, and more socially prestigious than breastfeeding.

## *Face to Face Situations*

On the other hand, Filipinos have an entirely different expectation when it concerns face to face 'sincerity'. In this situation promises and pleasing half-truths are important tools to avoid wounding *amor-propio*, because smooth interpersonal relations always take precedence over other values. Americans are flabbergasted when a Filipino 'yes' turns out to be a 'maybe', or when they are given a run-around instead of a straight 'no'.

One reason why Filipinos are not conscientious correspondents (not bothering to reply to RSVP invitations and then showing up, for example) is because for Filipinos the formal written context demands actual commitment and therefore sincerity in its fullest extent. Just as advertising, politics, and official negotiations in the American context calls for some suspension of expectations of sincerity, it is the face-to-face situation in the Philippine context that calls for a watered-down reading of expectations of sincerity.

It is a safe rule to say that a non-Filipino should take with a grain of salt what is promised in a face-to-face situation because Filipinos themselves always do. To establish the measure of sincerity, reiterate and obtain reconfirmation of the commitment several times, as well as act immediately to formalize and make irrevocable a verbal commitment. It is at this point that the person's 'sincerity' is tested, because if he hedges or does not act straight away, the promise and the 'yes' have been just to please you.

The Westerner is irritated because the Filipino will not come out and say 'no' to end the matter and save time; the Filipino is furious the Westerner cannot take hints and signals that the answer is 'no'. He has not said 'no' outright to avoid displeasing the Westerner and embarrassing him face-to-face with a 'no'. The Filipino thinks he is being considerate of the Westerner's self-esteem. What is offensive and what is considerate? It is merely a cultural interpretation.

## *The Importance of* Amor-propio

Why, you may ask, should the Filipino be so concerned about not causing offence? The importance of *amor-propio* (self-esteem) is one reason, but equally important is the kin-group world of Filipinos. Rather than value and stress individualism, each Filipino sees himself the centre of a kin-group universe; parents, grandparents, children, uncles, aunts, cousins, second cousins, in-laws, and *compadres* and *comadres*. In an open conflict, one wounds not just an individual but the whole kin group.

A quarrel between two people is not purely one between two individuals. A Filipino quarrel draws both kin groups into opposing camps. Notes Lynch on this point: '... when two Filipinos have a serious fight, there is much more at stake than when two Americans break off relations. This fact is, in my opinion, one reason why smooth interpersonal relations are more highly cultivated in the Philippines than in the United States.'

## *GUIDE TO SOCIAL SITUATIONS*

Face-to-face situations and Filipino etiquette wreak havoc on foreigners' expectations. Simple social invitations can cause irritation and misunderstanding and the classical hassles over 'sincerity'. If you bump into a Filipino friend in the street and casually mention you are asking some friends over for dinner and 'Why don't you come over too?' he will very likely say 'yes', but not take you seriously. The Filipino measure of face-to-face sincerity reads the situation as one in which you are probably just being polite and making a token offer. Chances are he will not show up.

You have to demonstrate the sincerity of an invitation made in this fashion by a telephone call or by sending a reminder through a mutual friend who is also going and who will assure the Filipino guest you mentioned unequivocally that he was expected. Otherwise, the Filipino verbal 'yes' in a casual face-to-face conversation is not deemed binding because, after all, your invitation is seen as just a passing thought, and not a specific desire to invite him.

Still on the nuances of Filipino etiquette, you must realize that Filipinos have a strong phobia for being placed in the situation of appearing socially pushy, of openly aspiring for social acceptance, or of being greedy. It is ingrained in their upbringing that avariciousness, gluttony, materialistic greed, self-aggrandizement and social climbing are to be sublimated; self-effacement, modesty, humility, generosity, selflessness are to be aspired.

In social gatherings, etiquette requires one to show up a bit late because punctuality may give the impression one is too eager for social acceptance and the feast. When the host asks his guests to eat, they never rush to the table at first invitation, they have to be cajoled, the invitation reiterated a few times, before they move slowly to the table. After dinner, guests will always leave some food on their plates, otherwise it will appear as though they were famished and had not been fed properly at home, or that the host had not provided enough.

If there is a dance, the host must keep trying to get people to dance. Such friendly insistence is the role of hosts. There will also be an overkill of food supply because it would be embarrassing to be caught short, and it is customary to offer guests who are close friends some extra food to take home. It is unusual to encounter Filipino guests who are extremely inebriated or behaving in disorderly fashion because to drink too much is greed and would seem as though one has never seen liquor at home; moreover, to behave rudely in public, drunk or sober, is taboo. Usually a companion will ease away one who shows signs of having had too much to drink before he causes a scandal.

If you are hosting a party, do not get peeved because you have to strain yourself getting people to the table to eat, for that is the role of host. Your Filipino guests are not treating you badly because they come late, appear reluctant to go to the table to eat, and have food on their plates after the meal; it's all part of etiquette. Filipinos are socially coy.

Small talk will revolve around people; that's the favourite subject because who you are is measured by who your family is, and who your friends and colleagues are. You are always seen in the context of your kin group. Questions during conversation may appear to be personal, but 'Why are you not married?' or 'How much did the dressmaker charge you for that dress?' or 'What does your father do?' are grist for conversation, placing you within a recognizable kinship context. Filipinos often ask foreigners the prices they have paid for local services because they feel real concern that foreigners may be getting 'ripped off'; they are ready to proffer advice on this.

At a dinner or party, some elderly folk may be observed in the background, their presence not readily noticed as they like to be in the shadow of activities. Usually they are parents or grandparents of the hosts and are always treated with great respect. It is customary to greet them and to make a point of bidding farewell to them before leaving. *Magpapaalam*, in Tagalog, stresses the etiquette of saying formal goodbyes to hosts and to elder persons in the house.

People in the upper middle class hire cooks as part of their household, therefore much of the food is not the hostess's culinary handiwork. Sometimes she may make the dessert. Compliments for the cooking, while welcome, will have less significance compared to a dinner which is the hostess's personal effort. The decor and flowers do involve the Filipino hostess's personal touch, and compliments are best directed there.

Guests do not necessarily sit in an alternate fashion of male and female, though some hosts may strive for this; instead guests tend to mix spontaneously and find their own seating arrangements and, depending on the outcome, the hostess then tries to get them to mix. The more common practice is for the host's wife and the guest's wife to sit together and the host and guest to talk together.

Unlike in some Western societies (e.g. Australia), it is not customary to bring candy or a bottle of wine for dinner; it would imply the hosts are not providing enough.

## Birthday Party Etiquette

1. Birthday parties are seldom sit-down affairs. Food is generally served buffet style.
2. Such parties seldom consist of friends only; they include kin.
3. People mix freely but tend to group according to generation.
4. Youngsters greet older relatives (*titos*, *titas*, *lolos* and *lolas*) with a kiss on the cheek (forehead if very old), a Filipino greeting. Older relatives acknowledge the greeting but do not return it.
5. Presents are not opened in front of guests. They are put aside in another room to be opened when the guests have left.
6. If you bring a driver, let someone know. The host is expected to feed your driver unless the party is an after-dinner one, in which case your driver should have his meal before you go to the party.
7. Close friends are given *pabaon* (some food to take home).
8. Dress is party attire.

## Filipino Dinner Party

A Filipino dinner will consist of soup, two or three courses, and dessert. Only water is served to drink during meals, although these days soft drinks are sometimes served. Wealthy, Westernized, sophisticated Filipinos may serve wine. Rice is the staple food in place of bread or potatoes. Filipinos eat with spoon and fork, using the fork to push the food into the spoon. At a more grandiose feast, food may also be served buffet style, in which case a greater variety is spread on a table and guests serve themselves with minimal formality.

If it is a family gathering such as a birthday party or a wedding anniversary, groups will break up according to generation or age, with the young children, the teenagers and unmarried, the married, and the grandparents tending to form separate clusters. Children are expected to stay in the background; they usually play together outside or in an inner room.

If the dinner guests include many non-relatives, there will still be family groupings, but the guests who are not part of the family enjoy special places, and quite often there is a polarizing of the sexes with women getting together and the men conversing in a group before the feast.

Filipinos enjoy dancing and many private parties culminate with disco dancing. Music—these days from a loud stereo system—is also part of the festive mood. On these occasions the men are offered gin, scotch or beer. Few women will drink alcohol, but for the men it is an exercise in machismo. However, while there is some pressure to be convivial and indulge, there is also the presence of the wives and some teasing to assure moderation. In rustic settings, the drinking may be a bit heavier, the men seem more inclined to prove masculinity, and the alcoholic beverages may be the local toddy (*tuba*) or its more potent, distilled form, called *lambanug*.

There is always the pressure of *pakikisama*, of being one of the boys, to get everyone to drink, and the trick, of course, is to be able to fend off subsequent offers when you feel you have reached your limit. And in spite of the teasing and the gentle jabs at *amor-propio*, most Filipinos smile and drink moderately.

## *Table Etiquette*

1. In urban areas, spoon and fork are used. In rural areas, people eat with the right hand. Food is picked up with the fingers and put into the mouth.
2. Food is usually served buffet style. Some families have a lazy susan on the table where the serving dishes are placed. A meal usually consists of rice and several viands. If there is a lazy susan, guests serve themselves.

3. In some well-to-do families, food is served to you by a maid. She brings the dish to each person and offers it to them, starting from the oldest person at the table. Guests are served first, those of higher rank before those of a lower position to them. Children of the host are served last.
4. Most families make it a point to eat together. Dinner is not served until all the members of the family are home.
5. Filipinos are big on desserts. Lunch and dinner are always followed by dessert.

## LIVING IN THE PHILIPPINES

Having become cognizant of the uniqueness of Filipino culture, one now steps into the nitty gritty of actually settling down in a house. Some things about a Filipino house in urban areas may seem strange to a foreigner. Walls are high, windows barred, and doors have locks on front and back doors. These have to do with security.

Sorry to say, porch climbers, burglars, and even armed criminals are part of the landscape. Leaving washed clothes overnight on the backyard line, or the garden hose and tools unsecured, are invitations to petty thieves. It will be just a matter of time before carelessly abandoned items in a garden are stolen.

The enclave-type villages in Manila's suburbs, surrounded by high walls and protected by uniformed security guards, are manifestations of the magnitude of the problem, and not signs of paranoia among suburban residents. Most city folk would be happy to dispense with these architectural features, especially since barred windows make firetraps, but they are there for a purpose. It is best for the foreigner to know this from the start.

The Filipino house is an expression of the Filipino lifestyle. Two swinging metal gates stand at the entrance on the street. These open to let the car inside. A door is built into one of the gates, to admit people without cars. In this door there is a small slot to allow someone, usually the househelp, behind the gate to see who the caller is before opening the door. The Filipino dislikes and discourages calls from strangers, door-to-door salesmen, creditors, and other undesirable pests within the privacy of his home; however, once identified and inside the gates, visitors are treated with the utmost graciousness and hospitality.

Most Filipino homes have a large living room because it is important to receive visitors well. There is a conscious effort to keep the public area where guests are welcomed looking its best. One illustration of this philosophy is the use of two kitchens, one with modern appliances looking like a page from *House Beautiful*, another called the 'dirty kitchen' at the back used for actual day to day cooking. A backyard for hanging washing and other unsightly odds and ends is distinct from a front yard carefully kept neat and abloom with flowers. The house is kept much as the Filipino runs his life, with an exterior front for public view, and an interior private space where the real living, warts and all, goes on.

## The Façade and the Inner Self

Filipinos distinguish between the inner self, called *loob*, and the outer self, sometimes alluded to as 'face' (*mukha*). The term *utang na loob* emphasizes clearly the debt is not considered superficial but an obligation of the inner self. Various expressions reveal this: one who cannot take pressure or risks is said to have a weak inner self (*mahina ang loob*); one who is daring and presumptuous is said to have a strong inner self (*malakas ang loob*); one who is generous and charitable has a beautiful inner self (*magandang loob*); while a person with a grievance or resentment says his inner self feels badly (*masama ang loob*). There is clear distinction between a person's public face and his inner, or true, self.

For the outer self—the façade—the Filipino applies such terms as form (*porma*), posture (*pustura*), face (*mukha*), composure, poise, artifice (*arte*), image (*papel*), dazzle (*pasiklab*), a show (*palabas*), a theatrical farce (*moro-moro*), a scheme to impress (*pakulo*), eye-

97

popping extravaganza (*pabongga*). These references show the mental distinctions Filipinos constantly and consciously make between a public 'face' and his inner self.

The architecture of a Filipino house expresses this distinction. Public areas where guests may be received are distinguished from private areas, and guests must always ask for permission before going beyond the living room to a private area, say to the toilet. There will be a sudden frenzy of cleaning and arranging before you will be allowed to enter the private spaces; these include the kitchen, bedrooms, den or study, bathrooms, backyard, and servants' quarters. The Filipino wants to be seen by others only at his best.

## The High Cost of Living

It is expensive, especially for foreigners, to live in the Philippines. Rent and petrol prices are higher than in America or Europe. Food, especially supermarket food, is also more expensive. All imported goods are subject to high tariffs, therefore many items such as imported foodstuffs, drugs and car parts are expensive. Over the last decade the inflation rate was awesome, running by conservative estimates to over 60%; but happily this has now stabilized to about 9%. Cars and appliances also seem to break down at a faster rate because of the weather and a lack of maintenance skills and spare parts. Most foreigners and all wealthy Filipinos send their children to private schools, where fees are high.

On the positive side are lower costs in labour and service, especially household help, and medical treatment. Professional services are generally excellent and less costly. Market food such as vegetables and fruit are both cheap and delicious.

A 1980 study by the American Chamber of Commerce estimated the costs of a typical, medium-level, American family's monthly expense at over 15,230 pesos. At the time the peso to US dollar rate was 7.3. In 1983 it was devalued to 14 to 1. The current floating rate is about 39 to 1.

## *HOUSE HUNTING*

In looking for a home, the foreigner should consider location first because traffic tangles, especially in Metro Manila, are legend, and entire mornings or afternoons are lost just getting from point A to point B. The heavy traffic is a fact of city life. The count, as of 1998, on registered motor vehicles in Metro Manila was 1,234,372.

The neighbourhood is one important consideration because of the gregarious nature of Filipinos, and the need to get along with the neighbours. Many vexing disagreements occur over garbage spilled by some neighbour's househelp on the street outside one's door, or neighbours constantly coming to use the telephone, or friction between two neighbouring househelps.

The need for security and protection against rampant burglary highlights the importance of location. Do not pick a house near an empty lot, or one near narrow congested streets, or in a dark, secluded area, without any fences.

Constant heavy rains during the wet season could easily cause flooding of home and streets, so study carefully the lay and contour of the property and the condition of the streets. If possible inspect during the wet season after heavy rain. It is easy to find yourself literally an island, in the height of one of Manila's seasonal floods.

Look for low areas in the ground floor and garden and for watermarks; make sure there is a good drainage system and that gutters and drainpipes are in good order, otherwise make arrangements to have these repaired and repainted. Check for possible leaks in the roof. Typhoons can rip loose roofing.

If there are street repairs being made on the main artery giving access to the house, be wary, because public street repairs can easily take years to complete and in the meantime disrupt all traffic in the entire block, creating a web of detours and clogged tiny side streets all around you.

Rent for foreigners is ridiculously high. This is because they are constitutionally banned from owning land in the Philippines, including a small package as a house and lot. However, a recent loosening of this restriction now allows foreigners to purchase condominiums (units). Furthermore, houses to let for foreigners have been specially built to suit Western standards and tastes, having amenities such as airconditioning and swimming pools that most Filipinos regard as luxuries.

Six months to one year rent in advance is commonly required. As of 1998, monthly rental rates in the exclusive Makati area favoured by expatriate businessmen are listed as 200,000 pesos for Forbes Park and Bel Air, 70,000 pesos, for San Lorenzo and for Magallanes, a minimum of 50,000 pesos. Residences located in neighbouring suburbs, but not inside subdivisions or villages that provide security service within their perimeters, command far lower rental rates. In most cases, the terms require a minimum of a year's rental in advance, aside from two months' deposit.

Rental arrangements may be between your business house and an agency; but more commonly they are made directly between landlord and tenant. You should remember the personalistic style of Filipinos and immediately establish a warm, friendly relationship. This makes requests for repairs and other business matters related to the house more effective. It is harder for the landlord to appear indifferent or irresponsible before someone he personally knows.

If you are satisfied with your new residence but would like to make some minor alterations, or add a fresh coat of paint, new curtains, shift the partitions, etc., try to get the landlord to assume supervision, if not costs, to save yourself disappointed expectations about workers' service. In any case, allow for more time than you would estimate for these small jobs; also, a margin of time from that promised and agreed upon to complete repairs because building schedules are definitely lax.

## Check the Basics

Foreigners accustomed to strict compliance with building codes will have to be aware of the lax building codes and enforcement of these in the Philippines. Do not, therefore, take basics for granted but check such things as electric wiring (faulty wiring is a major cause of fires in Manila), especially because foreigners are apt to plug in more electrical appliances than Filipinos (washing machines, dryers, vacuum cleaners ...).

In Metro Manila, the electric company (Meralco) offers both 110 volts and 220 volts; check the voltage carried in your choice of residence. Most modern homes carry both lines, in which case you have to know which type of socket carries which voltage. Mark sockets clearly, otherwise your 110 volt colour television just arrived from the USA will go *pffft!* in one push of the power button.

You should also be aware that, as in most third world countries, power failures are a frequent part of day to day life. These days, no previous warning is given. Power shut-downs, called 'brownouts'

101

because they are confined to pocket areas of a few city blocks, or one residential area, can ruin plugged-in electrical appliances because whenever power is restored a strong surge of voltage starts off the power. Some people unplug their appliances (refrigerators, freezers, airconditioners) and replug these only after power has been restored.

## Check Water Pressure

The newcomer to Manila should inspect the water pressure in the house first. Metro Manila's water problem goes back to the end of World War II when the city was left a shambles. Since 1945 water pipe installation and service have never caught up with burgeoning city growth. Almost half a century later, Manila's Metropolitan Waterworks and Sewerage System is digging up more streets than ever before in a losing battle to supply the, by now, more than 15 million Metro Manilans with running water.

In typical do-it-yourself fashion, Filipinos responded by using booster pumps to draw up water from the antiquated, narrow, rusty, leaky pipes and storing the water in tanks. Inevitably every house soon had to have a pressure pump as those without pumps got even less water from normal pipe lines. Despite these booster pumps, water pressure remains low, and few residential areas have adequate water flow at all times, especially during daytime peak usage hours.

Check the water pressure during peak hours if possible. Do not be satisfied with just turning on the tap in the garden or the ground floor; test the showers in the bathrooms of the topmost storey of your prospective residence. One good test is to turn several taps on simultaneously and then flush the toilet and see if water still flows through the tap. If the pressure is weak, you could find yourself stranded and waterless in a shower with soap on your face because someone in the kitchen turned on the tap, or someone else is watering the lawn.

Even with satisfactory water pressure provided by pumps, you will still have dry moments when the electrical power is shut off in regular 'brownouts' because your booster pump is run by electricity.

Typhoons have been known to knock down power lines while bringing torrential rains and floods, leaving homeowners knee-deep in water on the ground floor and in the streets, but with no water from the taps. A check on water facilities is therefore a must. You could be looking at a luxurious modern home with swimming pool and spacious marble-tiled bathrooms—check the water facilities anyway. If you live in a neighbourhood with low water pressure there is absolutely nothing you can do about the problem.

## Why Filipinos have Two Kitchens

The kitchen, a central part of some homes, merits inspection. In the Western context, the wife usually does the cooking and spends much time there, so kitchens flow into a breakfast nook or a casual dining-cum-family room emphasizing her central activity towards which the family gravitates. Filipinos, especially of the middle class and above, generally have a hired cook in residence, and the kitchen is merely the work area for a menial. Filipino kitchens are not brightly lit, well ventilated, cheerfully curtained, appliance furnished rooms, exuding the personality of the lady of the house.

If you intend to be master or mistress of your own kitchen, inspect the kitchen area, affirming that its location within the house, its size and amenities meet your needs.

Many Filipino houses, especially those owned by the wealthy, sport two kitchens; one for the lady of the house to indulge her culinary flair with modern appliances, another in some unobtrusive back part of the house, a smaller no-nonsense working space with gas cylinder fuelled burners for day to day cooking by the hired cook. The cylinder-gas fuel stove is useful because during periodic 'brownouts' your ultra-super electric oven and range become useless. A practical response to Philippine conditions, the 'dirty kitchen' relies on less sophisticated appliances because a hired cook does not really require time and labour-saving gadgets, but will very likely damage all your best new-fangled appliances, being unfamiliar with technical equipment.

## *Living with a Philippine Telephone*

It is also a good idea to check the telephone. In a city of more than 15 million people, the demand for telephones far exceeds the number of telephone lines available.

The telephone line you notice on cursory inspection may belong to the previous tenant who is having the line transferred to his new address. It does not hurt to get confirmation that the house does include a telephone. If it does, check if it is a single private line, because it is common for telephone lines to be shared, and nothing—but nothing—will aggravate culture shock more than having to share a telephone with one or more party lines.

While on the subject of telephones, the foreigner at the outset must appreciate the fact that this instrument is not the same simple device he is familiar with back home in Europe or Japan. In the Philippines it behaves in curious ways.

Even on a private line, crossed lines readily occur and introduce strange voices and muffled conversations at whim. To use the phone, you must hurdle all the numbers you are dialling without getting a busy signal along the way, a herculean task when dialling certain congested areas. Chasing someone through the telephone can take all morning and leave you exhausted. The phone goes dead when you most need it, and when it is working the telephone of the party you are calling is out of order, operating on some kind of Parkinson's law confirming the predictability of foul-ups.

As often as not, Alexander Graham Bell's invention works as intended, you solve problems in minutes, and walk on clouds feeling you have just won the Nobel Prize, satisfied all's right with the world.

It helps to have two telephone lines.

## *Keeping Dry*

A garage is essential because in the dry season the heat will turn your car into a high-firing kiln (you will have arrived at your destination before the airconditioning can cool it), and during the wet season it will get a constant soaking.

Heavy rains last several months, during which time you will have to get in and out of the house when it is pouring; so make sure you have a covered access from your car to the house. If you have a driver, see that the driveway and entrance to your house has a covered portion against the rain, to deposit you and your guests in and out of the house safe and dry.

## *Security*

Be security conscious in selecting and maintaining a house. The more streets that bound your house, as in corner lots, the more you expose yourself to outside invasion; the more secure-looking the houses that bound your lot (if these have private security guards it may help), the safer. Check walls, and gate, safety locks on doors, bars on windows, safety devices on sliding doors, and lighting fixtures, especially those that bathe the exterior premises in light.

It is largely the need for security that accounts for the wide acceptance of the 'village' subdivision concept. Upper and middle class Metro Manilans are pushed more and more into enclosed enclaves called 'villages' bounded by fixed walls or enclosures with entrances and exits controlled and checked by private security guards hired by the residents of the 'village'.

Each subdivision or 'village' has an association of members who try to minimize burglary and create a climate of personal safety within by limiting public access. Roads within the 'village' are usually owned and maintained by the 'villagers', so traffic flow and passage of cars are restricted to residents (who display stickers on the car windshield); guests in some 'villages' are required to register their entrance and exit. In most 'villages', the driver of the vehicle, even a taxi driver, has to leave his driver's licence at the gate and retrieve this on his way out.

The 'village' suburban lifestyle started in the late fifties and has mushroomed in the seventies partly because of Metro Manila's population explosion, partly because of vast business enterprise channelled to this area, partly in response to social needs. The village style has not totally checked the problem of security, and many residents in these villages are now periodically victimized despite a small uniformed and armed private army.

Security guards are members of agencies who provide the service on retainership. In practice security guards have proved to be double-edged swords; some have been involved in 'inside job' burglary, hold-up, and rape. A security guard is the perfect cover for a thief, as he has access to information of potential targets—number of people in a house, daily movements, when they are out of town, etc.

## Disadvantages of 'Village Style'

Another drawback of the village type residence is the polarizing of neighbourhood residents by economic class. Exclusively middle or upper class neighbourhoods naturally generate a keeping-up-with-the-Joneses race. It breaks up Philippine society into fixed socio-economic classes, inhibiting healthy community interaction between these various classes.

Outside the 'villages', the traditional Manila urban style of living had less obvious physical barriers between classes; it was common for a mansion to stand cheek by jowl with a modest bungalow and a decrepit shanty. The entire mixed neighbourhood availed themselves of the convenience provided by a tiny corner store called *sari-sari*, which sold cigarettes by the stick, a pat of lard, a cup of vinegar, and so on, all on accounts chalked on the wall. It is symptomatic of the widening gap within the socio-economic structure that the 'villages' have proliferated while the traditional residential areas have shown signs of decline.

## HOUSEHELP

Having settled in your new home, you are ready for close encounters with Philippine terrestrials. Few if any cope without some form of househelp and here your problem begins.

Geraldine Daigler, in a guidebook put out by the American Chamber of Commerce, entitled *Living in the Philippines*, writes: 'It is fair to say that at least one third of the problems faced by foreigners after the initial settling-in period revolve around the household help. Why? Because the average American or European is unprepared by training or background to handle a large household staff. Even a woman who has previously employed maids may not be aware of the intricacies of navigating in Philippine cultural waters.'

### The Tradition

The househelp has always been a part of Philippine life, as far back as existing historical records can take us. Spanish chronicler Juan Plasencia, looking into various classes in Tagalog society in the 16th century, noted that the chiefs or *datos* had two types of servants, one classed as serfs or share tenants (*aliping namamahay*) who serve 'their master, whether he be a *dato* or not, with half of their cultivated lands, as was agreed upon in the beginning', and the other the slave workers or chattels (*aliping saguiguilir*) who, unlike the first type, could be sold. There were quite involved rules governing the rights of both types of servants as well as delineating the powers of the *dato* over these and their children.

Rendering service to the *dato* or powerful person one is obligated to, as repayment for *utang na loob*, is still part of the dynamics of society. A young swain who aspires to marry his lady love in rustic Tagalog areas is (at least by traditional practice) supposed to render a year's service to the girl's parents, fetching water, chopping wood, and so on, to prove both his sincerity and industry.

It used to be the practice of tenant farmers to offer their young daughters or boys as servants to their landlords to whom they had incurred large debts, as a means of working off some of the payment. Even without debts many tenants still solicit househelp positions for their children with their landlords or other wealthy town or city people to whom the landlord may refer them. In its original context the Tagalog word for servant means helper (*katulong*). The Filipino reciprocity cycle traditionally functioned in this relationship between homeowners and househelp.

With roots in a loose form of slavery and maintained loosely by tradition, househelp enter, not as impersonal employees, but as part of a kinship group. However, this traditional relationship has broken down extensively and things are less harmonious. Except for taking in actual blood kins who ask wealthier relatives to see their children through school with the understanding that they will help around the household while living with them, few Filipinos are keen to get into a kinship cycle with the househelp as it involves too extensive an emotional and material drain on limited, dwindling resources.

Today, the househelp is referred to as a maid (in vulgar appellation, *atsay*); the masters of the house in turn are, to the maid, *señorito* and *señora*.

More and more, the relationship is becoming a love-hate one. Where by tradition the househelp would serve a household for years, even for life, these days the maid sees her job as transitory, a stepping stone towards a job as salesgirl, or waitress, or even hostess in a beer garden—until she marries a security guard or jeepney driver, to start a family in the city. The traditional practice was for the househelp to work and send money back to her family on the farm; it was the role of a good daughter or son. She also saved hard-earned money to buy a small piece of land to till, retiring after many years of service. Such househelp are now an endangered species.

The household that took in a househelp in turn assumed obligations to care for her, providing doctors and medicine in times of illness, gifts on special occasions, as well as her modest daily needs. If the family of the househelp needed help, the homeowner advanced some money or sent some clothing. The househelp who served as house cleaners, cooks, nannies (*yaya*), and gardeners were received with much good humour almost as part of the family.

Rising expectations have ensured that both homeowners and househelp are no longer satisfied with the traditional relationship. The relationship today borders on the professional and businesslike. A 1978 labour code of the Philippines governs employment of househelp (see page 242). While this code lists 60 pesos a month as the minimum wage for those employed in the Metro Manila area, the going monthly rate, as of 1999, is 2,000–4,000 pesos for house-maids and gardeners, 2,500–5,000 pesos for nannies (*yaya*), and 5,000–7,000 pesos for family drivers, with the exclusiveness of a residential area determining rates. Moreover, traditional relation-ships, watered-down versions, and confused applications of the old ways also accompany the code in practice.

Some Filipinos consider househelp part of the family, others treat them as chattels. Filipino society, however, frowns on anyone who maltreats househelp. Most homeowners just want the help to get the job done with a minimum of fuss and expense, but because the help stay in and interact with the family, personal relations come into play. The househelp in turn desire more than anything else warm, personal treatment. Drawing the line between generosity and abuse of hospitality creates conflict. Homeowners and househelp engage in a game every day where one tries to outpoint the other.

## Hiring Househelp

Filipinos hire help through word of mouth referrals. Many agencies exist, but hair-raising experiences do little to recommend these as the agencies have no real responsibility concerning the househelp's training, her abilities, and much less her character. Replacement of an inept new maid with another equally inept one becomes a futile exercise, and a long chain of househelp on trial only invites a

109

security risk. In the highly personalistic Filipino society homeowners prefer to inquire from relatives and friends who in turn consult their own help for suitable prospects.

There are two schools of thought about the hiring of househelp. One theorizes that if you get all your househelp from one region, one hometown or one kinship group, they will work harmoniously and you will be able to supervise a smooth working household; the other claims that if you get househelp who are of one kin group, they will cover up for each other, and you will not know what is going on in your own household until it is too late.

You may ask, but what could go wrong? Well, in a Philippine household the cook could be feeding the driver she fancies and all and sundry with your gourmet larder and best wine; your pantry could be thinned out by pilferage, your refrigerator made the watering hole of hungry househelp; your house may be the venue of swinging parties in your absence; the driver and the cook may be having a passionate affair you are blissfully unaware of, which means you will lose the now pregnant cook, as well as the driver who will flee the scene out of fear of reprisal from the cook's kin or a shotgun wedding. The maid may be flirting and entertaining all and sundry at your house—security guards, mailmen, garbage collectors, ice-cream vendors and, of course, ultimately burglars; that dearly-loved antique vase from grandmother may have been smashed months ago but nobody is talking, your pedigreed cocker spaniel bitch may be left loose fornicating with every stray mongrel, your best suit could be ruined by the laundress who was watching colour television while ironing in your bedroom; the house could have been abandoned because the entire household went off with the driver in your car while you were in the office.

All these scenarios have been drawn not from imagination or a B-rated movie, but from normal everyday happenings. Filipino homeowners will tell you they have never heard of, much less seen, a perfect househelp.

## *Tips on Managing Househelp*

A Filipino's notes on househelp would read along these lines:

Do not get two househelp who are from antagonistic regions, they will not get along. If they all come from one town they may take over your house. Try for a balance of kin and outsiders.

Provide separate quarters for male and female help, with females locked inside your house at night and males outside in the yard, protecting your premises. Inform them you frown on romantic fraternizing.

Provide separate food provisions for househelp and place your own family provisions in another pantry, preferably with a lock. Provide help with their own coffee to brew at their discretion; also types of food familiar to them, such as dried fish.

If the cook does the marketing for you, keep tabs on expenses and items purchased.

Give specific job assignments to each help and be sure each is aware of the others' responsibilities. It will avoid friction and buck-passing.

There is class distinction among househelp you should be aware of: drivers, for example, do not like to take instructions from maids, the cook may not like others meddling in her kitchen. It is advisable to clarify territorial domains.

Be alert for friction between the help: two may gang up on one and paint her black before you, without your realizing what it is really all about. When you begin to sense friction, make a thorough inquiry, but weigh in your mind the help you value most, then be prepared to dispense with the others or you will lose the one you value most.

A help who is well paid and who enjoys good relations with the homeowner may nevertheless be miserable because of harassment from the other help, and she will leave. If a help informs you she wants to leave she is signalling dissatisfaction, most likely because of friction with others. Get to the root cause so you can decide who must go.

Be watchful of loans and advances. Once the amount exceeds two months' pay, the help will lose all interest in work and you will find yourself with either an unpaid loan or a listless worker.

Anticipate increases and fringe benefits and grant these; otherwise they will be extracted from you by guile and you will not have gained any goodwill out of it. For example, the help will want to take leave when it is fiesta time in her hometown. If it will not disrupt your plans too much, it is best to yield; in any case, the chances are you will receive telegrams claiming her parents are seriously ill and she is needed urgently back in her hometown.

Provide varying privileges. Pay for travel expenses when the help takes annual leave. Aside from annual leave, days off vary from weekly to fortnightly, to monthly. Payment is usually monthly. Accommodation varies from a private room with colour television to floor space for a sleeping mat. Some are provided with uniforms. The annual bonus is a month's pay. Small gifts at Christmas, a dress, a purse with some money in it, are valued.

There are questions of days off, of receiving visitors, of what facilities and appliances the help can use for their own needs (for example the telephone) and countless day-to-day interaction involving the help living with you; the best approach is to apply your own personal rules and stick to these. There is no need to rationalize or explain your rules, simply explain clearly every chore and how you want it done, and put down your rules saying that is how you run your house. It is more important that your rules be known by repetition than justified and explained by logic.

While it is helpful to know the Filipino style of managing househelp, foreigners obviously have to apply a modified style. In the first place, most of the househelp who apply to work for foreigners have had some experience working for them, or else they are brought in to be supervised by someone who is familiar with the foreign home. Secondly, you will be charged more. Househelp working for foreigners expect better accommodation and facilities, more privileges, and better pay. A paternalistic relationship is not expected, unlike in a Filipino house. However, the values and dynamics still function with these househelp—they are Filipino.

## The Question of Privacy

The most important consideration in managing househelp is the personal relationship involved. It is the Philippine way. The expatriate will very likely feel he or she is never alone, and loss of privacy becomes the price paid for having househelp; the more help, the less privacy.

The Filipino help will not understand your strong desire for privacy, it is not a need that gets any kind of priority in Philippine society. Filipinos grow up with ever present human company: parents, sisters, brothers, aunts, nannies and other househelp. Human company provides strong emotional support, and most Filipinos crave human company every waking moment; especially so in times of personal crisis, illness, the loss of a loved one, but just as vital during times of joy, birthdays, graduations, receiving a special award, etc.

Gerda Koehler's unpublished thesis, 'Personality Needs of German Wives and Satisfaction with Life in the Philippines', quotes one interviewee: 'It bothered me to live with servants. My house is like a hotel lobby, the maids come and go any time, I always feel observed, I have no privacy in my own house.'

The feeling of being observed and overheard is more acute for English speaking foreigners because the househelp understand English and can hear everything. The only effective method is to keep certain areas, such as the bedroom, off limits except for a specific time for cleaning; and to teach the househelp to knock before entering, a custom Filipinos find superfluous.

## The Expatriate and the Househelp

Other cultural difficulty in coping with househelp have to do with feelings over treatment of househelp, how to relate to them. Foreigners feel the low salaries, long hours, difficult manual tasks, impoverished financial and physical conditions of the family of the househelp, and so on, contrast with their own lifestyle.

The question nags you—how do they live on what I pay them? The socio-economic gap is worlds apart. But with enough experience and time, practical considerations force a *modus vivendi*.

Soon enough you find yourself harbouring suspicions about the performance of the help. And isn't she consuming an unusual amount of coffee? Who was that strange fellow she was talking to outside the gate? Why can't she iron the shirts properly? They come with the territory.

Koehler's study quotes her German housewives' observations: 'I had to get used to the maids. I found it embarrassing to tell them if their work was not good enough for my standards. It was an insecurity on my behalf, how to treat them. But in the meantime, I think, I have learned that.

'My difficulty was how to make the maids understand what I want, how to make them work the way I would work. So 50% of the time I spent explaining, and then I found out it was still not done the right way.'

An arm's length relationship is advisable. It is not a good idea for foreigners to get into the Filipino kinship style which Filipinos in the urban areas are trying to get out of. While it may smack of social snobbery and class consciousness, it is not recommended you get into a 'good friends', first name basis with the househelp, because the househelp will very likely regard your friendship in Filipino kinship terms and expect more than you are prepared to offer, and ask more than you can possibly give. It will undermine your authority and you will lose control without your getting better service or appreciation. Within Filipino kinship, service to a friend is reciprocated with service, and a member of a kin group must be prepared to share what he has with those in need as well as offer advice on the most minute of personal problems, provide emotional support, and be loyal to a member, whether he is right or wrong. Filipinos distinguish between people within a kin group relationship and other Filipinos outside their own kin group.

## What You Value

Since perfect househelp do not exist, one has to lower expectations on performance and lay down rules. Peccadilloes will have to be overlooked as the price of inexpensive labour. If they were more educated and efficient, you can be sure they would not be househelp, there are more rewarding occupations. Do not trust, without direct personal supervision, your best suit to be laundered or ironed, or your heirloom dinnerware to be washed, or you may regret it. Remember that the value you put on some objects and goods will very likely not be grasped by the househelp.

*Item:* A foreigner stores in his refrigerator an exotic package of Gorgonzola blue cheese, a present specially flown over from Europe by a visiting friend. After dinner, salivating with anticipation, the foreigner asks for the cheese to be served, only to be told by the cook: 'Oh, that, I threw it away. It was full of mould, and really smelt awful. It was definitely off.'

*Item:* A homeowner treasures in a desk drawer an old World War II Japanese flag captured from battle, scarred with flame and bullet holes and grime. He nearly gets a brain seizure when he sees the maid dusting the dining room chairs with a portion of it. She had found this dirty, useless cloth and, thinking it made a handy cleaning rag, helped herself to a piece.

Those who have just come from the *barrios* will not understand your city life concern for security. Do not put your guard down with matters of your own house rules or the prevention of pilferage because once you relax your rules it is virtually impossible to restore them. A privilege voluntarily given once can easily become a permanent expected right.

## Househelp Pecking Order

Househelp have their own hierarchy and occupational personalities.

Cooks tend to lord it over the kitchen. Some have very fixed notions about one's palate and will not adjust to your taste, but most are gifted jewels who pick up recipes from other households and neighbours.

The nanny (*yaya*) is usually young and eager to play with the children. However, in her eagerness, she will transmit her values and ideas to the children too, and you may have your own notions about this, especially those that impart dependence, and the application of control and entertainment by oral myths peopled with other-worldly beasts, monsters, and demons.

The *lavendera* (washerwoman) is usually elderly, married, and likes to live out.

The all-purpose maid who does the housecleaning is the lowest on the totem pole; she tends to the others, answers the door and telephone, and feeds the dog.

## Your Driver

The driver thinks he is the cock of the walk in the household. He gets the highest pay, handles a sophisticated piece of machinery, drives about the city taking you to exciting places, talks for hours with other fellow drivers at the car park, comparing salaries and exchanging gossip about the employers.

Even if he is married with five children, he is very much the macho lover. His reputation is such, it is hard to say whether you have to protect the virtue of the female househelp against his seductive charms, or shield him from the ardent designs of love-starved maiden househelp.

The driver is a stickler about his off days and his mealtimes. If you find yourself in the car zooming with reckless abandon through the Manila traffic, it is probably past lunch or dinnertime, and you have neglected to give your driver a meal allowance. It is best to keep him well fed through meal allowances every time you are in a conference that will take time, or a shopping spree that will get you home later than the usual dinnertime. The driver also has his own notions about traffic rules and the overpowering influence of his employer over a mere traffic policeman. It's a good idea to set him straight on your views about traffic violations.

## Breaking In Househelp ... and Firing

Househelp learn their chores by doing, and develop job preferences as they learn.

All new househelp have to be instructed on their chores, handled best by actual demonstrations, especially in the use of cleaning equipment and cleaning agents.

Work out a system of being informed when household supplies have run out, otherwise you may find some chores have not been done for weeks because there was no soap.

Understand that Filipinos desire to please and do not want to reveal ignorance; do not take silence or a nod to mean they understood your instructions. It is a good idea to ask the househelp to repeat your messages over the telephone; it seems patronizing and time-consuming, but it will save heartache until you know his/her capabilities.

Invariably there will be dissatisfaction with a househelp's performance, or personality clashes that require your terminating some househelp's employment. This is best done quickly and irrevocably. The tactful approach is to say that it is the househelp who expressed dissatisfaction with your household ways ('you are obviously unhappy with us here') and give severance pay.

It is not offensive to inspect the departing househelp's luggage; and, in fact, the househelp may prefer this to avoid post-departure accusations.

Bear in mind that tears or expressions of anger should be avoided in these instances of termination—the person suffering from *hiya* and wounded *amor-propio*, and her kin as well, may consider retaliation.

## *Advantages of Help*
Once you are aware of this perspective with househelp, you will discover the advantages and why everyone in the Philippines not merely 'puts up with it' but often cannot survive without it. Conversation among Manila ladies invariably touches on househelp, inquiring if anyone knows of a reliable one because the one she had just left her, or how marvellously efficient someone who has been working for years is.

Having househelp will give you much leisure time. After a while you may no longer have the energy to fetch a glass of water from your own fridge or hunt for the newspaper yourself. Your house could function without your lifting a finger.

The expatriate housewife then enters a second phase of cultural adjustment. She will feel she is not needed. Since few expat wives pursue a career in the Philippines, she has to fulfill herself in other ways outside the home. The challenge is in the socio-cultural scene where women are most active. There are civic projects and diverse women's organizations. For personal development there are art groups, theatre groups, garden clubs, soirees ... countless activities made possible by the leisure time provided in having househelp.

## PRIVATE AND PUBLIC SPACE

You may be puzzled over the contradictions concerning private and public affairs of Filipinos. Filipinos, for example, are always personally clean and well groomed, their houses and gardens well-tended and attractive—while just outside the house, garbage is strewn on the sidewalks just adjacent to the house gates. Public sanitation is appalling despite ubiquitous red- and yellow-attired Metro Manila Aides perpetually sweeping.

The Filipinos make a distinction between their private space and the public space. Filipinos do not think of public space as being a shared community asset which must be cared for and respected by all: that concern is passed on as the task of government. Filipinos have not really come to terms with their relationship with the government (taxes, jaywalking, littering, etc.). Without the physical presence of a traffic policeman, for example, traffic lights and signs are not obeyed seriously. A person in authority is respected, but an abstract depersonified sign will very likely be ignored.

People throw their trash out in the streets for the garbage truck to pick up. At times a neighbour's househelp throws garbage on the neighbour's pile, causing conflict. Garbage collectors often pick up garbage on certain corners, creating huge, unsightly and unhygienic mountains. The solution, the foreigner will promptly suggest, is to have nice clean garbage bins in the streets for easy collection. The trouble is that, in the Philippines, bins will disappear. Pilferage is rampant. Even heavy iron manhole covers are stolen, not to mention hundreds of metres of live wiring from electric poles!

While stealing is considered immoral and a crime, 'borrowing' and pilferage are rampant. Mail delivery is not very reliable for this reason. Traditional Filipino kinship patterns develop a lax attitude about helping oneself to a family member's goodies. Reluctance to share is considered extremely stingy. If you do not want something to be touched in a Filipino home then you have to put it away and lock it in a private drawer. Otherwise there will be members who will help themselves. This is why you are advised to be vigilant about pilferage from househelp. Sharing is the custom. Buying cigarettes by the stick has proved a convenient practice among Filipino workers because one is not required to pull out a pack which must be offered and shared with everyone around.

The confusion regarding public space is also said to be part of the reason for traffic snarls. Driving in Manila requires full concentration. Vehicles of all sorts will come from the most unexpected directions. The feint-and-jab style of driving is the accepted means of crossing clogged lanes. A driver is considered to have initiative if he bypasses queues, blocks traffic by double parking while you are shopping, climbs sidewalks, and gets you to where you want to go by fair means or foul. Philippine driving is aggressive and competitive, and a foreigner who has been learning about Filipino smooth interpersonal relations will wonder where all that SIR went.

In questions of public space, of public property, and also of corporate property, ethical standards and a confusion of how to cope with these situations has led to pilferage, anarchy, and chaos. Filipinos simply try to muddle through these situations the way they do with traffic, and the foreigner will just have to take it in stride.

# Chapter Six

# DOING BUSINESS IN THE PHILIPPINES

## *The Nationalist Factor*

Foreigners have been coming to the Philippines for business reasons since at least the 10th century. Archaeological evidence reveals vast quantities of Chinese Tang and Sung pottery (as well as Thai and Cambodian) in the country. The Arabs, too, who in the process introduced Islamic beliefs, came to trade. Europeans trod on Philippine shores in search of spice. By the end of the 16th century, the Spaniards had turned Manila into an entrepot, shipping (via Mexico through the famous galleon trade) Chinese silk and porcelain to Europe, on the return trip bringing Mexican silver which was much in demand in Asia. Later, in 1856, the British sent vice-consul Nicholas Loney to Iloilo, and in no time he had carved out a market for highly industrialized British textiles despite the fact—noted at the time by Loney—that there was at least one loom in almost every home and, by his estimate, Iloilo had 60,000 looms in operation.

Obviously, the Americans, too, envisioned business prospects when Dewey sailed into Manila Bay uttering the famous words: 'You may fire when ready, Gridley.' In 1946, immediately after World War II, Americans enjoyed equal rights to exploit natural resources through a controversial amendment to the Philippine constitution, one of the conditions stipulated by the US for granting the then Philippine Commonwealth an independent republic status.

What do these cursory bits of history have to do with the price of copra in the Philippines? This particular historic framework must be taken on board by the contemporary foreign businessman because it takes into account the historic tension between foreign business and national interests in the Philippine landscape.

From at least the postwar years, a nationalist ideology has been used by Filipino businessmen to do battle with the heavily fortified bastions of foreign business interests. Filipinos will tell you that it has been only in recent times that some of their countrymen achieved top executive positions in foreign-owned business establishments. Top positions were traditionally the exclusive domain of expatriates. Until at least the late 1960s, news media was largely owned by foreigners, while most of the heads of religious institutions and schools were aliens.

A nationalist ideology was highly instrumental in giving Filipino businessmen and professionals equal footing in their own homeland. This nationalist ideology has direct roots with the 19th century movement of the Filipino clergy to gain its rightful place within the Spanish frailocracy. National hero, Jose Rizal, traced his own nationalist outlook to this movement.

One must never ignore such a strong and deep-rooted Filipino national experience. In 1954, for example, a law was passed nationalizing the retail trade. This was aimed at removing Chinese control of the retail trade. In subsequent years political pressure was brought to bear on two foreign-owned companies in public utilities, the Philippine Long Distance and Telephone Company (PLDT) and the Manila Electric Company (Meralco), forcing the owners to sell out to two select Filipino families who now wallow in their respective monopolies.

You must always read up and be constantly aware of any existing or new legislation directly affecting your business. Some points of the Nationalist Business Credo are given on page 245.

## *Minding Your Business*

Nationalistic barriers aside, businessmen who come to the Philippines will find the climate conducive to multinational commerce as the structure is basically Western. Facilities for conducting commercial enterprise are up-to-date, English is the business lingua franca, and low-cost labour is in surplus. Skilled labour, in fact, is one of the biggest exports of the Philippines, accounting for vast exchange earnings (from money remitted to their families by these expatriates) that have helped offset the lopsided balance of payments. It was once called a 'brain drain', but now is more kindly seen as one way of easing unemployment, and a dollar earner to boot.

The previous Marcos regime pulled out all stops, rolled out the red carpet, and provided all manner of incentives, to make foreign businessmen welcome. While a bit more circumspect in the light of the Marcos experience, the Estrada government maintains a practical policy of attracting foreign investment to the Philippines.

The Asian Development Bank is based in the Philippines. An Asian Institute of Management has been providing young business-men in the Philippines and neighbouring countries with training, studies and insights on professional skills in international business.

The foreign businessman will therefore find the Philippine business environment attuned to contemporary business systems and practices. Big business houses have all the sophisticated furniture and paraphernalia of modern commerce.

However, the use of the most advanced communication tools are only as good as those using these tools and expatriates may find themselves going bananas when the periodic power failures shut down the airconditioning and much of the office activity, traffic snarls make the simple matter of getting from one office to another just a suburb away an entire morning's ordeal, telephones do not function smoothly, the mail takes forever to get delivered, and the urgent shipments and packages get entangled in a limbo of paperwork at customs.

A good business location is essential. Always consider the traffic factor. The original downtown Manila (across the bridge where Plaza Goiti and Escolta are) lost its prime location because of heavy traffic. The business centre moved to Makati which has now become even more hopelessly choked by traffic.

The style of doing business in the Philippines is casual and leisurely. Things may seem to go speedily and smoothly at the top level (although decisions are seldom forthcoming without much hemming and hawing) but at the level of implementation things move much more slowly, as each person who could possibly have a say must demonstrate that he/she has a say. A go-between can assist in pushing through these human barriers; certainly you will keep your blood pressure at a safe level if you let subordinates and assistants negotiate through the people channels.

Decision making is confined to the top. Access to the top is only through intermediaries in informal social meetings which then move to a more formal discussion though still in a social situation such as a luncheon. Even at the top, the chief executive may not want to commit himself and he may say a proposal has to go to a board or committee. Chances are this is another way of saying 'no', because the depersonalized board or committee can be utilized to take the blame for the negative action.

In meetings, a lot of the decisions have already been threshed out through informal discussions and go-between assurances of support. Usually, by meeting time, most are aware of the positions of the members on a sticky issue. The decision to approve or knock back a proposal has very likely been made in backroom caucuses.

Lay the groundwork for such meetings and count votes or else chances are the decision will be negative or deferred for further study. It would be most unusual for boards and committees to approve something presented at the meeting itself, cold turkey. Usually the members want to be apprised not only of the merits of the proposal, but the who and why—that is, they have to know the people behind the proposal. The *who* takes the highest priority.

## *The Business of Telling Time*

Whatever the case, things take time. There are long luncheon meetings and *merienda* discussions. Pleasantries make up the bulk of communication throughout all these. Small talk about the personal welfare of everyone takes up much of one's time. The foreigner is constantly eyeing his digital watch to read the time, while his Filipino partner or client is admiring someone's gold rolex watch and inquiring where he bought it. Talking about time will hasten the end of the meeting but very likely defer any decisions until the next one. Bringing attention to the gold rolex watch as an ornament of high status, on the other hand, could score the right points and warm the climate for a positive decision. A vast repertoire of jokes wins arguments. That's business in the Philippines.

Dress at the executive level is a business suit. Ladies may also wear appropriate dress—after all, being female is not a professional disadvantage despite the overt macho manners of male executives.

While American style informality is the pattern at the office, access to top management is always barred by a private secretary and you should have the initiative to get into a hospitable relationship with these guardians of the powerful. Chatting them up a bit and getting on a first-name basis with them (they will still call you by your surname and office title or at least 'Mr') can make communication with top management smoother.

Business cards are useful only to give your address and telephone number. Verbal agreements should be formalized with a written contract or memo.

While not formally associated with the business, wives of executives play a social role with employees and fellow executives. Most wives take this behind-the-scenes role seriously.

## *The Personalized Business Style*
In a highly personalistic society, business is always best done on a face to face basis in a warm, pleasant atmosphere. Where you think time is gold and want to get to the point immediately, the Filipino beats around the bush, talking about mutual friends and family, exchanging pleasantries; only when the right and proper climate is established can the negotiations be considered.

No matter what the final result, the discussions should always end cheerfully. You may feel you are wasting time talking about other people and sundry matters, but to a Filipino, cultivating a friend, establishing a valuable contact and developing personal rapport are what make business wheels turn.

Culture shock in business strikes when you try to get familiar business equipment, and the recognizable organizational structure, to work in the way you have made it function countless times 'back home'. You start pushing buttons, but nothing happens. The human factor makes everything different. This is why we stress repeatedly that it is essential to know something about Filipino values, history, and the kinship structure. The business pace slows down considerably in the Philippines and you must provide generous margins for timetables, deadlines, and work schedules.

## Dealing with the Bureaucracy

Alas, inevitably in business one has to grapple with the bureaucracy. Paperwork is the hallmark of dealing with officialdom; dozens of signatures are required for the entry through customs of the simplest items sent to you by air cargo. The Filipino approach to the problem is to make use of the office personnel who have developed skills in moving through this paper jungle.

Whether it is as simple a matter as getting you a driver's licence or the car registered, your mental health and your blood pressure will benefit from delegating the chore to someone in your office who is paid to negotiate through a sea of desks, who knows each one there enough to smile and exchange light banter and get signatures through. Needless to say this person should enjoy your office support by being the one who personally delivers Christmas gifts to his desk-bound contacts.

On many occasions nothing moves without *lagay*, a euphemism for a small bribe which some scholars prefer to call 'persuasive communication'. While there are those who claim it is not necessary to produce an 'unsolicited but expected' token of appreciation for services rendered, others say it is the only antidote for the agony of inaction. *Lagay* is officially and publicly considered illegal and immoral, therefore applying 'persuasive communication' is unspoken and unwritten. Desks of some petty clerks or bureaucrats are said to be left open in the expectation of something dropping in without anything being said.

Graft and corruption have been issues discussed since time immemorial. Political elections under the postwar republican form of government (1946–72) were invariably contested on these issues. On occasion, official statements and clean-ups surface to confirm that corruption is alive and well, but for all public purposes graft and corruption are terribly illegal and horribly immoral. It's what has been called split-level Christianity and the double standard. But then crime and graft exist in other societies, other cultures too. In fact, in various big payola and kickback scandals, the givers, who may even be considered the real corruptors, were big multinational firms mentioned in congressional investigations in other countries but never prosecuted.

The Marcos martial law regime proved a high water mark for this unhappy practice, creating, overnight, corrupt billionaires who are still very much with us. Various government institutions, including the judiciary, have yet to recover some modicum of rectitude. The loss to the country has been estimated in the billions of US dollars. No one has been charged and convicted for the sins of the Marcos years. Despite the trauma, the general published opinions of various agencies and professionals is that this sad state of affairs has not markedly changed after Marcos to this very day.

## *Tips on Graft*

Anyway, the graft that does not exist is practised in the imagination of some interviewees who describe their fantasies along the following scenarios:

A traffic policeman flags you down for a traffic violation, and asks you who your 'lawyer' is. The reply is supposed to be the face of the hero on the peso note you are prepared to hand out, such as 'Osmeña' (50 pesos) or 'Roxas' (100). Misplacing three 100 peso notes inside the driver's licence you present to the traffic cop is cheeky but has been known to work. Foreigners often can get off if they can manage to appear firm while dropping the name of some important official they claim to know.

Kickbacks, commissions and rebates are handled by middlemen. The go-betweens, sometimes called 'influence peddlers', convey the requirements of their powerful friend. There is no way of really knowing where the money goes, therefore if you are dealing with really 'big bickies', strive to go direct. An informant tells us the method is to pay a courtesy call to the top official after determining amounts from the go-betweens. On leaving, place the large envelop on his desk, and when Mr Big feigns ignorance you say it is just a small gift. Another informant tells us his style is to come with an attaché case full of paper goodies which he leaves, case and all, in the office of Admiral Big. You need quite a number of disposable attaché cases without identifying initials if you do a lot of business.

## Don't Get Personally Involved

On the subject of go-betweens another informant draws a scenario that brings into play General Big's mistress, called number two. The legitimate wife is above all this naughty business, but a mistress, who is not supposed to exist anyway, makes the ideal go-between. Everyone knows she represents him, and thus the non-existent number two can vigorously engage in non-existent corruption.

In split-level Christianity and double standard morality, happenings below the surface are never spoken about and are never admitted to exist. Foreigners may suffer shock confronted with talk about *tong* or *lagay* or 'rebates' and 'commissions'. One cannot be too wary, so never get into dirty water personally or directly.

## What Makes Filipino Businessmen Run

On a happier note, for normal legitimate business affairs with Filipinos, bear in mind a fundamental difference in motivation. Anthropologist Lynch identifies three things that motivate and control Filipino behaviour: social acceptance, economic security, and social mobility.

Material considerations, profit or remuneration take secondary importance to family interests and job satisfaction. Titles of office proliferate in the Philippine scene for this reason. Western corporate titles generally carry with them responsibility and some autonomy, whereas despite a wider distribution of titles and job classifications, Philippine organizations are highly centralized with a wide gap in distribution of monetary rewards. Arce and Poblador (*Formal Organizations in the Philippines: Motivation, Behaviour, Structure, and Change*) attribute this to the Philippine society's shortage of trained top echelon managers, the practice of giving titular status as a reward in place of material monetary compensation, and the fact that most companies are owned by a single family or a handful of kin group individuals.

Another observation made is the high degree of explicit judicial rules spelling out offences, with clear procedures on punishment for infractions, hearings, and adjudication for each case. Punishment appeared the stronger mode of control, not material rewards or other inducements. This system is very likely due to the need for smooth interpersonal relations and the avoidance of damaging *amor-propio* with explicit rules. All foreseeable situations have been depersonalized and face to face, personal interpretation of disciplinary action is avoided because implementation is ministerial.

These observations should be sufficient to again point out what by now will be obvious. Philippine business houses are run differently from Western ones, and the style is determined by the Filipino kinship values; *hiya, amor-propio, pakikisama, utang na loob* and smooth interpersonal relations come into play. There is no getting away from these. You have to be aware of them. Because terminating a regular employee's service involves a sense of *hiya*, government policy requires 'just cause' or authorization of the Department of Labour who will ask for documentation of 'just cause'.

In business circles, the traditionally emancipated Filipina, while highly efficient, is careful to project her femininity, and you must remember the society's reservations about overt intimacy, touching and so on, between the sexes. Her friendliness and mild flirtation are part of her bag of attractive assets and her 'smooth interpersonal relations' or *pakikisama*, so do not get carried away.

## Government and Business

One special characteristic of the Philippine business scene is the vulnerability of commerce to government restrictions, laws, and their implementation. As one saying goes, 'For my friends everything, for my enemies—the law.' Your business could suffer while another's prospers by the passing of a law, or a new government regulation, and what may seem to you its arbitrary implementation. It was common practice for business houses to have politicians looking after their interests, and in the past some family power blocs fielded members in politics to expand their commercial base. It is the old kinship expansion system in the national arena. Inversely, various politicians built economic empires.

Personal interaction, socializing, establishing contacts in government sectors and in the media as well as in business are important not only to get your viewpoint heard but also to learn early of governmental changing moods. President Marcos's rule by decree after 1972 intensified the uncertainty of planning business since a variety of changing statutes and regulations seriously affected business. While a more stable system has now been restored by the Estrada government one must still be ever alert to that bane of doing business in the Philippines: fickle government regulations.

Do not keep your eye only on the business, keep your eyes and ears open for government rules, changing government moods, and the movements of competitors.

## BUSINESS ETIQUETTE

### Lunches and Dinners

1. Business lunches and dinners are usually arranged personally over the telephone and only confirmed by the personal secretary.
2. Be sure to address people by their titles (e.g. Congressman Cruz, Attorney Jose). The cue must come from *them* to address them more informally.
3. The inviter pays. If you are a guest and therefore not paying for the meal, it is expected that you do not order the most expensive items on the menu, unless your host insists.

4. It is customary to have a drink before sitting at a dining table.
5. A pleasant atmosphere and minimum formality set the tone. Business is not usually discussed until after a convivial tone has been established, usually after soup has been served.
6. Dress for the venue. It is never wrong to wear a *barong tagalog*.

## Official Parties

1. Acknowledge invitations, even though Filipinos tend to be lax in replying to RSVPs. Telephone follow-ups should be done a day or two before the event. If hosting, have your personal secretary 'chase' guests to confirm a day or two before the occasion.
2. In a formal occasion, seating is arranged. There is usually a head table for the VIPs.
3. Prominent guests are usually introduced.
4. A guest speaker is often the highlight. Light entertainment may be provided. Don't be surprised if important guests are asked to sing, and do. If you have a good voice, make capital of it.
5. Dress is semi-formal unless otherwise indicated.

## Office Etiquette

1. Dress at the executive level is a business suit for men and a smart dress or suit for ladies.
2. Reprimand employees privately. Be gentle and end with some show of personal concern for the family to make the person feel still part of the team and that criticism is not personal.
3. Coffee breaks—remember that Filipinos enjoy coffee breaks and must have their *merienda*.
4. Filipinos like to greet one another. Make it a point to do so.
5. It is customary to give gifts to employees at Christmas. It is also the time to show appreciation of other people you have regular dealings with, e.g. the post-office boy, security guard, doorman, as well as good customers and clients, through token gifts. Gifts range from hampers or company giveaways to plain calendars.

# Chapter Seven

# HISTORY, CULTURE, CHARACTER

Filipinos, it has been said, are Malay in family, Spanish in love, Chinese in business, and American in ambition. History intervened in the evolution of Filipino cultural life, intruding with a heavy hand on critical occasions, for better or worse irreversibly affecting Filipino character. A look at the biography of Philippine culture can help explain why Filipinos think and act the way they do today.

## The Stone Age: Hunters and Food Gatherers

The oldest human remains is a 22,000-year-old fossil skull-cap found by Dr Robert Fox in the Tabon Caves in Quezon, Palawan. The find raised some questions because earlier theories placed a Negroid-pygmy group (Aeta) as the first people in the archipelago. As no archaeological evidence puts the Aeta (Negrito) groups in the Stone or Metal Age context, their presence remains a mystery.

Earlier evidence of man in the Philippines are stone tools associated with fossils of now extinct animals such as giant tortoises and stegodonts, in Cagayan. The early peoples were nomadic hunters. As recently as 1971, a band of 27 people who called themselves the Tasaday were brought to world attention because they appeared to have been a stone-age, food-gathering tribe living totally isolated in the rainforests of South Cotabato on Mindanao. Stone Age people were probably both hunters and food gatherers.

Neolithic technology, which came about 6,000–500 B.C., influenced cultural development. The new polished tool permitted efficient clearing of forests, leading to the emergence of agriculture, the domestication of animals, boatbuilding and pottery; and, naturally with these, a more sophisticated socio-political system.

## The Metal Age: Bamboo People

The Metal Age, which followed some 700 to 200 years B.C., further broadened cultural horizons. That ever-handy tool, the *bolo* (which has become part of the English language) emerged; and with this tool, bamboo was exploited efficiently.

Filipinos have been described as a bamboo people: they live in bamboo houses (walls, posts, floors are of bamboo); they sing and dance with bamboo (*sinkil* and *tinikling* are famous bamboo dances, and the bamboo organ of Las Piñas is a national treasure); they cook with and eat bamboo (cooking containers, drinking cups, knives, are of bamboo and bamboo shoots are a favourite dish); they hunt and fish with bamboo spears, poles, and traps.

*Tinikling, a bamboo dance popular in lowland rice-growing areas, symbolizes the Filipino prancing in and out between clashing cultures, Western and Asian.*

## A Filipino Myth on the Origin of Man

Not surprisingly, the classic Filipino explanation of origin is that man came from a bamboo. According to the myth, a bird was incessantly flying between sea and sky, unable to find a place to alight and rest. Applying intrigue, it sparked a quarrel between the sea and the sky. It told the sky that the sea had designs of rising and drowning the sky, who replied it would fight such a move by hurling rocks and islands to hold the sea down, a statement the bird conveyed to the sea, provoking it to lash waves at the sky. The sky retaliated with rocks until, weighed down with islands, the sea no longer proved a threat. The bird then alighted happily on a protruding rock.

While it was resting, a bamboo node washed ashore and nudged the bird's feet. The bird shifted a little. The bamboo nudged its feet again, and again the bird shifted. This went on until the bird in anger pecked at the bamboo, breaking it open. Out of this bamboo node emerged the first man. From the second node emerged a woman.

135

Obtaining permission from the gods, the couple had many children. All grew up idle, doing nothing to help their parents until the father in anger picked up a stout stick and threatened to beat them all, sending them scampering in terror. Some ran out of the house, others fled to the bedroom, a few cowered in the living room, some hid in the kitchen, some among soot-covered cooking pots.

Those who entered the bedroom sired the chief and *datos*, those in the living room became freemen, descendants of those who hid in the kitchen became the slaves, while those blackened by cookpots produced the Aetas. From those who fled the house never to return, descended all the peoples in other parts of the world.

This story, with variations, is widely disseminated, recently even used as a modern dance theme. The original couple (in some versions the male is called *malakas* or powerful, the woman *maganda* or beautiful) lingers in a niche in the collective memory.

Traces of the Metal Age lifestyle are still visible among various cultural minority groups, such as the T'boli of Mindanao and the Ifugao in the Mountain Province. Both these groups still retain small-scale metal-casting work.

In the Metal Age, pottery reached a high peak of development, and evidence of the potter's skill can be viewed in various national repositories and private collections. Weaving flourished; a back-strap loom, tie-dye, textile art is still in practice among existing cultural minority groups. There was much interaction between tribal and regional groups. Archaeological evidence reveals dissemination of pottery wares and designs throughout the archipelago.

## Age of Trade and Contacts

Foreign traders made their way to the archipelago from the 10th to the 16th centuries in a period known as the Age of Trade and Contacts. The Chinese sailed in their junks, bringing porcelain and silk in exchange for deer horn, *trepang*, and beeswax. Chinese trade was so extensive porcelain ware has been found in every nook and cranny of the archipelago, inside inaccessible caves in Palawan, among the Kalinga and other tribal groups in the Mountain Province, beneath coconut groves in Laguna, and other ancient gravesites on countless islands—even under the main street, church grounds, and basketball courts in Santa Ana, Manila. The hundreds of thousands of porcelain pieces, some going as far back as the Tang dynasty (10th century), but mostly Sung and Ming ware (12th to 16th centuries), speak of extensive contact over hundreds of years.

## Chinese Legacy

The Chinese contributed many things: culinary techniques, of course, such as sautéed dishes, and a variety of rice cakes and noodles; various cooking implements such as the wok (*kawa*) reveal their Chinese origin in the names used for these.

The corner retail store and vegetable gardening are Chinese. The Filipino family structure was reinforced by the more rigid authoritarian Chinese style, and traditional Filipino families still make clear distinctions between family members, including from the oldest child and on down the line to the youngest, with names that are Chinese. The eldest son is addressed as *kuya* by the other children, the elder sister as *ate*; their authority as well as responsibility over younger siblings are clearly defined.

When the Spaniards moved in to colonize Manila, they encountered a Chinese settlement there, and throughout the Spanish period the colonizers, while paranoid about the Chinese, made use of Chinese skills. The Chinese were master craftsmen, helping in the building of churches and large homes, and furniture makers as well. The oldest church in the country, San Agustin in Manila (16th century), still displays a choir loft and chairs carved by Chinese in Canton; Chinese stone lions guard its churchyard walls. Much of religious imagery of the Spanish period, called *santos*, bear Chinese influences such as Chinese cloud formations in paintings and carvings, and almond-shaped eyes in wood and ivory faces of saints.

The Chinese in the Philippines were, in turn, influenced by Filipino life. Those who married Filipinos had to accept the matrilineal along with the male line in family structure. The Chinese are patrilineal, Filipinos bilateral. For the Chinese male migrant who had little family in the new land, the dominance of his Filipina wife's family became absolute.

Chinese who acquired wealth in the Philippines often intermarried with those of the ruling class, forming a Filipino-Chinese *mestizo* (half-caste) class who became active members of the elite. Various prominent Filipino figures such as the national hero, Jose Rizal, the revolutionary leader, General Emilio Aguinaldo, and a statesman who served as the president of the Commonwealth, Sergio Osmeña, carried Chinese blood in their veins. Corazon Aquino claims Chinese lineage.

The Spanish had a paranoid attitude towards the Chinese, and their centuries of rule were marked by sporadic but systematic massacres of the Chinese. Western colonial exposure has developed anti-Chinese sentiment among some Filipinos. Chinese migrants to the Philippines, mostly impoverished and willing to endure hardships for a decent life, are seen by some Filipinos as an aggressive economic threat, pragmatically sublimating every aspect of life for business ends; others merely see their lack of knowledge of Philippine languages and frugal lifestyles as manifestations of inferiority. Derisive and derogatory references to Chinese are often heard among Filipinos; folk stories, plays, and songs usually portray the Chinese as sinister or comic figures.

## *Advent of Islam*

The Arabs, at about the same time as the Chinese, had also come to trade. Even before Islamization of Arab countries, the Arabs frequented the ports of China. But Islam gave the Arab lands wealth, population, culture and a sense of empire. In the Southeast Asian region the founding of Malacca, followed by the conversion of its

*A village mosque in the southern Philippines, a symbol of the Islamic influence that filtered in just before the Spanish colonizers intruded.*

leader in 1414, spread the influence of Islam among the Malay peoples, reaching southern Philippine shores around the 14th century.

Islam remains a very dominant influence among Muslims in the southern Philippines, a factor that unified the kinship groups in the area to resist colonization by Spain effectively and strongly for four hundred years, and put up a strong resistance to American colonization. Although a small minority within the Philippine population (about 5%), the Muslims have added cultural character to the nation. The Filipino Christian majority today express pride and admiration over the Muslims' warlike defiance of colonization.

139

Throughout the Spanish period, however, Muslims launched raids on Christianized coastal areas, terrorizing inhabitants, pillaging and plundering, capturing victims for Dutch slave markets. Christian Filipinos invoked the protection of saints, the favourite being Santiago Apostol, known to the Spaniards as Santiago Matamoros ('killer of Moors'). Tall, mute watchtowers stand on some Philippine coasts as relics of turbulent days when the threat of Muslim raids was ever present, and the alarm cry '*Hay Moros en la costa*' (the Moors are coming) entered Philippine colloquial expression.

The Spanish reinforced antagonism against the Muslims by popularizing and disseminating their own Islamic phobia, through plays (*moro-moro*) depicting the battle between Christians and Moors in Spanish history, as part of Philippine fiestas. They called Muslims in the Philippines 'Moros', identifying them as the Moorish infidels who conquered and ruled Spain for centuries until the Reconquest.

A schism lingers between Christian and Muslim Filipinos. The Muslim separatist movement (MNLF) and the government's military reaction are manifestations of this antagonism which continues to be exploited by sinister men for their own devious ends.

The age of trade and contacts brought about a confluence of ideas and culture. Neither was it merely the outside exerting influence on the archipelago, as the Philippines also became the conduit for influences funnelled outwards to the Pacific.

Trade generated much domestic exchange between the various inhabitants of the archipelago. Vast quantities of porcelain diggings in recent years attest to the extent of inter-island domestic trade and cultural exchange. Gold jewellery of this period reveal highly sophisticated craftsmanship unequalled in many parts of the world.

Malay culture flourished during this era also. Only the accident of history and colonization in the late 16th century placed Indonesia under the Dutch, Malaysia under the British, and the Philippines under Spain and subsequently the United States, branching the Malay peoples off into three different directions.

## *The Spanish Period*

The last of the traders to sail into Philippine harbours was Magellan's fleet, halfway through the first circumnavigation of the world. After this 1521 landing, other Western voyagers arrived. The Portuguese, the Dutch and the British were to be regarded as invaders by dint of Magellan's touchdown on Limasawa and 'discovery' of an archipelago already inhabited for hundreds of thousands of years, its inhabitants in more recent centuries enjoying trade with the Arabs, Chinese, Siamese and neighbouring Malay peoples. The Philippines fell under the aegis of Spain for the next four hundred years, until 1898 when she ceded the territory to the United States for 20 million dollars indemnity, in a treaty in which Filipinos had no part.

When Magellan landed he encountered the standard kinship feud between two chiefs. In order to ingratiate himself with one of them, Rajah Humabon, and to display the military invincibility of Spain, Magellan offered to destroy the group under Lapu Lapu. It

141

was a fatal error. Magellan's men miscalculated the tides, the shore was out of reach of Spanish naval guns, and troops had to wade in knee-deep water in heavy armour, sitting ducks for the fast moving multitudes armed with spears and swords. Magellan was killed, the survivors lost face with their host who, seeing the vulnerability of the Spanish, butchered as many as he could lure to shore, causing the survivors to scuttle one ship, and flee in the remaining two.

The interesting note here is the kinship rivalry, a characteristic still very much a part of the Philippine social landscape. Chances are Lapu Lapu and Raja Humabon continued their feud.

Regionalism is still a Filipino characteristic. When a person is dissatisfied with a group he belongs to, he simply walks off and forms his own group. Professional and social clubs proliferate because groups tend to splinter. Even among Filipino communities abroad there are usually at least two rival camps. This failure of Filipinos to unite solidly towards a common purpose has been described as *banda uno-banda dos*—a town having two rival musical bands instead of pooling the best musical talents of the town into one band.

The Spanish, and later the American, colonizers exploited this built-in divisiveness to conquer the Philippines. In post-World War II years the political system of the independent republic evolved had less to do with ideology and more with political conflict and elections along rival kinship lines. Families of the elite in many towns and provinces can trace running rivalry over several generations.

## *The Santo Niño*

While Magellan was in Cebu, Humabon's wife (described as the 'queen' by Magellan's chronicler, Pigafetta) became enamoured of a small statue of child Jesus and this was given to her. Forty-four years later, in 1565, when Spain sent a fleet under Legazpi to colonize the Philippines, a Spanish soldier searching for booty in Cebu found a statue of the Holy Child 'like that made in Flanders' in a box showered with flowers. Was it the image left by Magellan?

Whatever the case, Legazpi's entourage recognized it as a Christian icon, and used it for religious conversion. The statue is still in Cebu.

Devotion to the Santo Niño is very much alive today. The Ati-atihan of Kalibo is a fiesta paying homage to this image of the Christ child. It has become almost a cult; a strange one since devotees venerate not Christ the God-man who died on the cross, but Christ the child. At fiesta time the Santo Niño image is threatened with immersion if it fails to bring rain. Once a year, throughout the country, Santo Niño images are bathed and dressed.

## The Virgin's Statue

Legazpi subsequently destroyed and captured Manila. Here again a sailor, wading, chanced upon another image among *pandan* roots, this one of a lady. It was declared miraculous, and this wooden sculpture has been enshrined in Manila's Ermita church as Nuestra Señora de Guia. Some contend the image is the Chinese goddess of mercy, Kwan Yin; others see it as a native idol; still others claim it is a Christian icon of Portuguese origin, pointing to the name Nuestra Señora de Guia as Portuguese and to a similar image in Macao.

The statue is described as made of two local hardwoods, the face and carved hair (false hair was later added) having oriental qualities. The statue is offered as evidence that Christianity preceded the coming of the Spaniards; in fact Legazpi had reported an encounter with a Japanese wearing a 'theatin' cap (worn by Christians) and who on query affirmed he was indeed a Christian named Pablo.

These two religious images, linked directly with the Spaniards, reveal that Christianization at the outset did not totally cut itself off from pre-Christian links and beliefs. Other images introduced developed cults, the Marian one being strongest, with the Virgin of Antipolo and the Nuestra Señora del Rosario (La Naval) drawing large followings during the Spanish reign. A folk Catholicism evolved which the historian, Phelam, described as one permeated with 'an atmosphere of the miraculous and the supernatural'.

*In the Feast of La Naval, one of the largest and most popular in traditional Manila, the image of Nuestra Señora del Rosario is carried on a large* carroza *through an important sector of the city. It celebrates a famous Spanish naval victory during the Spanish period.*

## Christian Legacy

Christianity was the major force introduced by Spain to Philippine culture. It was instrumental in many important changes. To Christianize Filipinos, Spanish missionaries drew them into population centres. A programme of putting potential converts 'under church bells' (*bajo las campanas*) was vigorously pursued, thus leading to the formation of towns with the church as their centre, the populace within hearing distance of its bells. The bigger the bells, the larger the community.

*The Church of Miagao Iloilo shows strong Spanish influence and the local adaptation and emergence of a Philippine style in church architecture. Photo by Jane Kempe.*

The typical Philippine town is still very much as conceived and structured by Spanish Christianization: a central plaza, the church at one end, *municipio* or government house at the other, houses of leading citizens on both sides. The plaza complex, in fact the creation of urban towns, is a Spanish contribution.

## The Fine Arts

Christianization led to the building of churches, an architectural concept previously unknown in the Philippines. The heavy massive stone structure was grandiose, conceived for permanence on a huge scale—very different from pre-hispanic Filipino art forms which viewed rituals, and art forms related to these, as transitory. Building the churches and the priest's quarters (*convento*) beside them not only developed urban architecture, but introduced new technology and materials for building. Christian rituals called for interior decor, statuary, paintings, and liturgical music. Out of these religious needs developed Philippine fine arts, architecture, painting, sculpture, a Western form of music, and theatre.

145

*San Roque, venerated in many Philippine towns as a guardian against epidemics. Photo by Jane Kempe.*

Countless churches throughout the Philippine countryside (especially in Laguna and Ilocos) speak of the development of Philippine church architecture. Philippine religious statuary and paintings likewise evolved a national style and these artifacts are now avidly collected and displayed in museums. Painting took such strong root that secular painting in the form of portraiture and landscape soon graced wealthy homes. By 1884 two Filipino painters in Europe had bagged top honours there, Juan Luna gaining the coveted Prix de Rome, the highest single art award of the time.

The large Spanish colonial house evolved from the humble indigenous house, the nipa hut. The classic nipa hut, still in use, is built on stilts with entry via a ladder located in the middle, a main receiving-cum-living room area, inner bedrooms, and a space extending out of the kitchen, called a *batalan*, for water storage and messy chores. The Spanish colonial house enjoys the same layout on a much grander scale, using more permanent bricks and tiles, a wide entrance also in the middle, a grandiose staircase, and a spacious living room (*sala*), with the water storage area adjoining the kitchen called *azotea*. Both houses are single storey, but elevated from the floor, the bottom area used for storage. Both houses permit air circulation through high ceilings and openings in walls.

The nipa hut and the Spanish colonial house were functional responses to the physical environment. High-pitched roofs funnelled the flow of heavy rain, windows (in the Spanish colonial house, of capis shell, in the nipa hut, bamboo lattice work) blocked off the glare of light but allowed the free flow of air. The Spanish colonial house shows how Filipinos adopted Spanish ideas and technology, shaping these towards their own special needs.

Grafting of Western Renaissance 'fine arts' into Philippine culture enriched and expanded Filipino aesthetics. Then, art was the product of an anonymous villager with a flair for pottery, basketry, weaving or carving; now, the individuality of the artist gained prominence, and he signed his name to his works. Then, art was transitory— wooden carvings, flower and leaf offerings to be left to the elements and quickly reclaimed by nature; now, the Spanish introduced stone for church structures and sculpture, a written literature, and oil paints, materials devised to keep a work of art as long as possible. Art on a grand scale is also a Spanish legacy; much of pre-hispanic Philippine art was of modest size, in contrast to the towering stone churches, the larger than life religious images, or the painted murals.

Philippine literature, which in pre-hispanic times was oral, acquired the Latin alphabet. Growing from religious literature, it developed in the vernacular the Passion of Christ (*pasyon*), religious plays (*sinakulo*), and Christian-Moor dramas (*moro-moro*), and then developed metrical romances (*awit, corrido*). By 1891 a Filipino named Jose Rizal had published two political novels that shook the Spanish colonial regime in the Philippines.

In many ways, Christian Filipinos picked up Spanish culture, selectively absorbing what suited their lifestyle. Music, dress, dance, cuisine, ceremony, bureaucracy, political ideas—none was borrowed in pure form; transformation was essential. Even Spanish terms adopted in Philippine languages acquire different connotations, if not totally different meanings. Spanish for 'certainty' (*seguro*) in Tagalog and Pilipino means 'uncertainty' (Filipino for 'certainty' is *segurado*), and the Spanish for 'philosopher' (*pilosofo*) has come to mean, in Filipino, a 'sophist'—not a wise person, but a 'wise guy'.

## *Roots of Hispanization*

The Spanish *compadrazco* system was adopted but harnessed by kinship groups to gain powerful members. Catholicism was accepted but with emphasis on ceremony, fiesta, and the miraculous powers of many saints. A sociologist noted that Protestantism which preaches direct dialogue with God did not enjoy the same rapport with Filipinos as the Catholic practice of relying on the intercession of saints, because Filipinos always operate through a go-between!

Strict modesty became part of Philippine sexual morals. The chaperone was very much a part of Philippine courtship practices before World War II—sweethearts were never left to themselves during courtship. Many Filipinos still frown on a boy and a girl dating without a chaperone or other girls and boys. Spanish missionaries had strong views against nudity. Modest dressing remains a strong trait of Christian Filipinos. Even among men, it is not the practice to walk about totally unclothed, even in a public shower.

However, Filipinos were not fully hispanized, unlike some Latin-American countries. Spain did not rule the Philippines directly but via Mexico. Many of those who came to colonize the islands had gained from a previous Mexican experience or were half Mexican. The galleon trade which served as the Spanish connection to the Philippines for more than two and a half centuries commuted between Acapulco and Manila, bringing Mexican influences rather than pure Iberian ones. Mexican words for 'father', 'mother' (*nana, tata*), 'market' (*tiangui*) and plants introduced from Mexico still linger.

Instead of teaching the inhabitants Spanish, as in Mexico (which resulted in the total demise of the Nahuatl language), the Spanish missionaries learned the Filipino language in the mission area to which they were assigned. This has been interpreted as a scheme to keep Filipinos ignorant, because the Spanish language would have opened Western civilization to Filipinos. Be that as it may, the argument only underscores the tremendous intellectual and cultural contributions of Spanish intrusion into the archipelago.

## *Friars and Filipinization*

The zeal of the Spanish missionaries placed them in outlying areas, establishing parishes and building churches, while Spanish government officials were content with living in the comfort of Manila's old walled city (Intramuros), making a fast fortune on the galleon trade. The Spanish clergy became the power in provincial parishes as well as a political force in Manila. The Filipino elite (*principalia*) sought to channel their children towards the most prestigious seat of power which was the clergy, considering higher political office would have been denied them anyway.

The rise of a Filipino clergy ultimately led to a clash between the Spanish friars and the new class of Filipinos who challenged the Spanish colonizers by becoming not merely Christian, but priests. Three Filipino priests were falsely implicated in a mutiny in Cavite and publicly executed in Manila's Bagumbayan (now Rizal Park).

149

The 1872 martyrdom, known in history as 'Gomburza', was the turning point. The Philippine national hero, Jose Rizal, only 11 then, was profoundly affected by it, his brother Paciano being a student of one of the priests. Rizal's famous second novel was dedicated to the three martyred priests: '... as you may or may not have been patriots, and as you may or may not have cherished sentiments for justice and for liberty, I have the right to dedicate my work to you as victims of the evil which I undertake to combat.'

The first political conflict between Spain and the Philippines began with the growing Filipinization of the clergy, strongly resisted by Spanish friars who refused to share their status, power, wealth and the 'good life'. With Filipinization of the clergy held in check by Spanish friars, the Filipino elite turned towards secular areas.

A wealthy native class emerged around the mid-19th century, manifested by the rise of colonial houses in major towns. Banking was institutionalized, landed estates carved out, sugar produced and tobacco factories erected. The educational system boasted a university and an observatory. Children of the elite were sent abroad to master professions, to be identified, upon their return, as *illustrados*. A national political identity took shape.

## The Filipino Emerges

The sense of nationhood was therefore another effect of Spanish colonization. In the beginning, inhabitants of the archipelago were called Indios. The term 'Filipino' was first applied to Spaniards born in the Philippines, to distinguish them from those born in Spain; the 'luckier' ones (to their minds anyway) born in Spain stressed the fact that they were 'Peninsulares'. The Spanish as well as the Chinese *mestizos* were soon enough also identified as Filipinos.

The Filipino *illustrados* agitated for reforms, using their erudite training to demonstrate that Filipinos were the equal of Westerners and capable of representation in the Spanish Cortes, if not of self-government. The artistic triumph of two Filipino painters, Luna and

Hidalgo, were acclaimed by the *illustrados* as triumphs of the race. The reform movements were viewed as subversive.

The inevitable radical swing from legitimate demands for reform to a clandestine movement to overthrow the colonial government by force, finally came about when the Spanish persecuted and exiled Jose Rizal, a highly respected *illustrado*, doctor of medicine, artist, poet and novelist. A secret society called the Katipunan, founded by a former warehouseman from Tondo, Manila, spread among the masses. The Spanish era had played itself out and armed struggle followed. Filipinos claim to be the first nationalist movement in Asia, the first to have launched an armed revolution against Western colonizers in Asia.

The sense of nationhood, the identity of the very word 'Filipino', emerged out of the Spanish colonial experience. Previously Filipinos thought in terms of kin groups, of *barangays*, and of language groupings such as Tagalog, Visaya, Pampango, etc. The Filipino *illustrados* who voiced their national identity wrote in Spanish which was understood by other *illustrados* from different regions of the country. At first, reform appeals were directed at Spaniards in Spain, but when this failed, the propaganda campaign shifted to Filipinos in the Philippines, arousing a national identity and a pride in their ancient culture and indigenous roots. 'There are no tyrants where there are no slaves,' Rizal exhorted his countrymen.

## *Philippine Independent Church*

Christianity, Spain's contribution to the Philippines, was not so much a theological conversion as an emotional one adulterated by indigenous values and beliefs. Pageantry emphasized a surface Catholicism. While succeeding in mass conversion, some friars also served as very poor personal examples, and Filipinos today think of the friar as a person who enjoys the good life. A long, lazy easy-chair is known as friar's chair (*silya de fraile*). Loose morals among some Spanish friars were responsible for literally fathering the

151

*mestizo* class in many parishes. No less than Mrs Imelda Romualdez Marcos has traced her ancestry directly to a Spanish priest.

*Illustrados* attributed the evils of colonization in the Philippines to a 'frailocracy'. Rizal, his family a victim of land conflicts with the clergy in Calamba, attacked the abuses of the Spanish friars in the Philippines. Marcelo del Pilar, another Filipino propagandist noted for the bite of his pen, also directed satirical attacks on what he called the 'monastic supremacy in the Philippines'.

This conflict between the friars and the nationalists, with roots in the frustrated movement for the Filipinization of the church of 'Gomburza' days, has created a strong schism within Philippine Catholicism. One major splinter group is the Philippine Independent Church under Gregorio Aglipay, a Catholic priest who split with Rome to found a Filipino Catholic church. Many Christian towns often have two churches, one Catholic, the other Aglipayan. Filipinization conflicts still surface on occasion in various Catholic institutions dominated by Western clergy.

Thus, Christianity in the Philippines is very much a humanized one, the earthy lifestyles of the Spanish friars vivid in the history and memory of Christian Filipinos. A priest who loves wine, good food, and picaresque humour has greater acceptance than the silent ascetic or the fire-and-brimstone demagogue.

## *Looking Behind Those Spanish Names*

Most Filipinos have Spanish-sounding names like Ramon or Leonora, and surnames, such as Gonzales and Romualdez. These names were adopted only in the mid-19th century, to be exact in 1849, by a decree issued by Spanish Governor Narciso Claveria, who observed Filipinos had no surnames to distinguish them by family. Surnames were created to help trace degrees of sanguinity, facilitate legal and civil cases, and check on taxation, personal services and the draft.

Surnames were given to people who registered throughout the land. In the Bicol region this alphabetical register was implemented alphabetically by towns. Surnames starting with A were given to those in the provincial capital, while surnames starting with B and C applied to coastal towns, and so on. Townspeople chose their surnames from pages allocated to their town. One can speculate on a person's family origin from the first letter of the surname.

Previous to this decree, Christian Filipinos acquired religious surnames, but there were so many Cruz, de la Cruz, Santos and de los Santos, that the identical surnames were as confusing as having no surnames. Iberian surnames among Filipinos, therefore, do not indicate Spanish ancestry.

## *Start of Urban Life*

Urban Filipinos adopted the Spanish colonizers' style and manners; aristocratic airs, social snobbery, the self-importance of public office, disdain for manual labour and the obsequiousness of underlings lingered among some middle-class and upper-crust Filipinos. The Spanish obsession with honour was identified with the Filipino respect for self-esteem, and the Filipino term now in use, *amor-propio*, is Spanish. Probably the Tagalog term *pagpapakatao* (acting with human dignity) represents the original value of self-esteem. Filipino wariness of offending self-esteem doubtless alerted them to the exaggerated touchiness of Spanish *amor-propio*.

Urban living split Filipino culture. The vast majority of Filipinos lived (and still do) in the *barrios*, but the creation of towns and cities diverted many to urban living. The Spanish *urbanidad* means civility and courteousness, the urban way of living. Around the mid-1860s, a bestseller, *Urbana at Felisa*, was written by a Tagalog priest, Modesto de Castro, in the form of letters which counselled the rising Filipino middle class on manners and morals. The book was a success not only because it filled a need for Filipinos to understand urban living, but more because it married these urban manners and etiquette to existing Filipino kinship values. The book helps mark the point when Western city ways were 'Filipinized' by Filipinos.

## Barrio *Life*

From this point onward urban and rural lifestyles have enjoyed a continuing cross-culturization. About 70% of Filipinos live in the *barrios*, mostly farming and fishing. Life in the *barrios* moves with the sun and the seasons; seconds and minutes are irrelevant. Running water is found in streams, not in the plumbing. Electricity has only recently begun to invade *barrio* life. Doctors do not exist and medicine is still very much the domain of the traditional herbal healer. Cash is not as extensively used as traditional barter.

At *barrio* level life seems timeless; changes occur very slowly. Economic life lies at subsistence level. *Isang kayud, isang tuka* is the Tagalog expression describing chickens left to fend for themselves, who 'scratch and peck' for sustenance. The drudgery of the seasons is relieved only by the occasional fiesta, and only if the *barrio* has saved enough to afford one.

Traditions are nurtured in the *barrios*. The family unit is the hub, and order is maintained by kinship pressure rather than law enforcers. The educational level is barely beyond fourth grade because school is far away, books are expensive, and farm hands needed. *Barrio* folk are born, married and die without leaving their *barrios* except for visits to the nearest town at fiesta, or to buy and sell produce.

A few leave to work in the cities, or to further their education. Some are youths, restless and seeking excitement. An estimated 25% of the population in the cities who live in shanties that encroach on private or government land are migrants from the *barrios*. They are called squatters, and their homes *barong-barong*.

## *An Astonishing Contrast: City Living*

The cities are the receptors of modernization. Metro Manila leads: in industrialization, bureaucratic institutions, commercial establishments, mass media, universities, hotels, museums, bookshops, hospitals, millionaires, prostitutes, criminals, policemen, firemen, artists, movie stars, airline pilots and street-sweepers.

Metro Manila is the seat of government. International conventions are held here, world-acclaimed performers appear in its concert halls. Western influences enter in the form of visiting foreign experts, returning young intellectuals, fresh from American and European universities, professionals trained in the latest practices abroad, a flood of world mass media information, and importation of the most advanced technical equipment and gadgetry from all over the world.

Those totally in love with the Western culture are called 'Brown Americans'; in Spanish days they were the 'Dona Victorinas', after a character in one of Rizal's novels. The malady is referred to as a 'colonial mentality' or 'blue-seal mentality' in reference to the preference for imported cigarettes with the foreign blue seal tax. In the days before military rule, when political ideas and parties proliferated and vied in the open market of ideas, a movement for American statehood was quite active. The love affair with the gross side of Western life has also been dubbed 'Coca Cola culture'.

*Avant-garde* art, rock 'n' roll, Hollywood movies, drag racing, fast foods, video games, a cornucopia of consumer goods and ideas pour into Manila and filter down to other cities, towns, and ultimately, perhaps only as conversation, reach the *barrios*. The contrast between urban and rural life is easily glimpsed by looking at a ritzy revolving restaurant with wine and food prices that represent several months' income to common folk and comparing these with the simple nipa hut and the repast of *barrio* living—a little dried fish, some vegetables and rice. The price of a car is beyond a peasant's wildest dreams. Doctors who try to practise in the *barrio* are invariably frustrated because they are viewed with suspicion, and cannot avail themselves of medical facilities, while the medicines they prescribe are beyond the financial reach of their patients.

Yet a continuing dialogue does exist between urban and rural life, and the foreigner who observes closely the assimilation and sifting of Westernization into the *barrio* level will be rewarded. Tension between Westernized town and traditional *barrio* is what

155

makes the society Filipino. There is something of the *barrio* lad in the most sophisticated Filipino, while the *barrio* peasant is readily transformed into an urban model.

## Bridging Rural and Urban Living

One sociologist has observed that the city's slums serve to prepare rural migrants for urban life, the period in the slums being a transitory lifestyle with the support of kinship values and traces of rural ways to ease him into city life. Those who make the transition ultimately move out to be part of the urban society; those who fail either return to their hometowns or stagnate in the half-way community of the slums. The *barong-barong* (shanties) are an ugly side of urban life, but if we accept Laquian's study, *Slums Are For Living*, they serve as a cultural bridge to urbanization.

Urbanized living—theatre, art galleries, stock markets, penthouse apartments—is irrelevant to *barrio* living, but criss-crossing between these two extremes are gradated scales of urban and rural ways. Househelp straight from the *barrios* work in posh apartments, while the transistor radio puts urban voices and thoughts directly into the *barrio*. A highly efficient nurse in Makati Medical Hospital is very likely supporting peasant parents in the *barrio* who made sacrifices to get her through school. The link is personal and direct.

Barong-barong *or shanty. Pieced together from scavenged bits of wood, iron and newspaper, these dwellings are architectural feats in themselves.*

## *Rural Folk Make Western Things Filipino*

The process of absorbing Western influences into indigenous roots has become the Filipinizing process. Cultural symbols the nations identify as Filipino are mostly Western ones which have undergone transformation through the folk process. Alien things absorbed by urban Filipinos do not really become Filipino until they are assimilated by rural folk.

For example, the national costumes—the *barong tagalog* for the men and the *balintawak* for women—are Western clothes which have received folk touches in the process of assimilation. The *barong tagalog* is a 19th century Western shirt, worn outside. (Some historians claim the Filipino 'Indios' were required to wear Western shirt-tails out to distinguish them from Spaniards in early days.) Through the use of Philippine materials (*jusi* or *piña* during the Spanish colonial period), embroidered with native folk motifs, it acquired a native character.

Philippine dances were Spanish jotas, rigodons and polkas, becoming 'Filipino' by undergoing rural transformation. Antique religious statuary (Santos), highly prized by collectors today, are precisely those with folk touches. Today, a western vehicle, the US army jeep, given folk touches of paint and other decor, is the expressive Filipino vehicle called the jeepney.

This tension and interaction between urban and rural, between outside influences (mostly Western) and traditional roots, is the Filipinizing process. If the extremely urbanized neuro-surgeon is Filipino, so too is the soil-rooted faith-healer. Such contradictions are resolved by shades of personalities countlessly running the range between both extremes. You could surprise a highly sophisticated Filipino millionaire eating dried fish and *bagoong* in the privacy of his kitchen, or a *barrio* boy gyrating to the latest dance steps. Tradition and change are the stuff of Filipino culture.

Though less visible, ideas, values, manners and morals, organizational systems, new skills and techniques, beliefs, aesthetics—all undergo a similar process. It is what created a body of religious beliefs called folk Catholicism. The foreigner experiences a peculiar form of culture shock in the Philippines because he encounters the Western urban façade and begins to communicate and deal along pre-conditioned Western ways, only to discover these do not mean quite the same thing nor work the same way. 'No thanks' from a Filipino need not mean 'no'. It often means 'Are you just being polite? Ask me again, prove you mean it, and I will say "yes".' The American 'okay' and the Filipino 'okay lang' have different nuances.

## *The Hispanic Connection Makes the Difference*

The Spanish period was thus a significant watershed. It gave birth to the Filipino of today. It is possible to evaluate how the Filipino would have evolved had Spain not forced itself into *barangay* life. Islam's influence in southern Philippines helped people there to resist Spanish rule, preserving the Muslim Filipino lifestyle, from the stately Maranao to the proud Tausog. Among physically inaccessible minority groups such as the Manobo and T'boli in Mindanao, the Hanuoo in Mindoro and the Tabganwa in Palawan, as well as among the Ifugao, Kalinga and Bontoc in the Mountain Province, where neither Islam nor Spanish culture penetrated, one can study prehistoric Philippine culture minus the Spanish transfusion.

## *Jose Rizal: Filipino Model*

The Spanish conquest that imposed itself on Philippine life grafted influences which took root and flowered into a unique Filipino culture. A new breed of Filipino emerged, a pupil who surpassed the master, demanding equality, critical of its weaknesses. The best and the brightest of this new Filipino was Dr Jose Rizal.

Whether the foreigner wishes to learn Philippine history or not, he cannot escape the Rizal presence. There is a monument to him in practically every town and plaza in the country; his likeness hangs in many schoolrooms and appears on the two-peso bill, the one peso coin and postage stamps. Every main street in the country is named Rizal, as well as an entire province, Manila's most important park, a theatre, and even mundane products like cement, beer, matches, cigars. A nationwide organization called the Knights of Rizal, with chapters in various parts of the world where Filipino communities prosper, thrives with no other purpose than to perpetuate Rizal's teachings. Various folk-cult groups revere Rizal, some placing him among the pantheon of Christian saints. Rizal's monument in Rizal Park, where his bones are also interred, is under the vigil of guards of honour in full dress, and every important visiting dignitary lays a wreath in homage to him. Anniversaries of his birthday (June 19) and his martyrdom (December 30) are national holidays. Volumes have been written about him, operas and movies made of his novels. Hardly any serious conference on the state of the nation or Philippine culture convenes without someone quoting some line from Rizal.

All other national heroes may cause controversy and dispute; Jose Rizal is the one figure whose ideals and personal example enjoy genuine national admiration. To know Rizal is to understand the Filipino model. He represents the Filipino's highest aspirations.

Rizal was born on 19 June 1861, in Calamba, Laguna, of parents who belonged to the local elite harbouring some Chinese ancestry. A highly educated woman for her time, Rizal's mother became a victim of the *guardia civil* and the *alcalde* injustice that so terrified her, she confessed to a crime of which she was innocent; she was imprisoned but subsequently absolved. The incident left a deep impression on the sensitive boy. His brother Paciano, a student of one of the three martyrs of the 1872 Gomburza affair, inculcated in his younger brother nationalistic pride.

Rizal's family valued education. His home boasted a vast private library, rare in those days when the friars limited available books to religious tracts. The precocious child grew up to be a brilliant scholar, attending Manila's Ateneo and the University of Santo Tomas, where he studied medicine, philosophy and literature, taking two courses simultaneously and winning literary awards. With Paciano's help, he enrolled at the Universidad Central de Madrid, specializing in ophthalmic surgery. Upon obtaining his degree, he served as assistant under two eminent European ophthalmic surgeons, Louis de Wecker in Paris and Otto Decker in Heidelberg.

As a student in Spain, he became involved with Filipino students who agitated for Philippine reforms, in what has come to be known as the Propaganda Movement. In Berlin, at age 26, he wrote his first novel, *Noli Me Tangere*, the first socio-political novel describing Spanish and Filipino life in the Philippines with realistic accuracy. He annotated a new edition of Antonio de Morga's 1609 *Sucesos de las Islas Filipinas* to show with what admiration a distinguished Spaniard viewed Philippine prehistoric culture. His second novel, *El Filibusterismo*, explored violent revolution as a solution to Philippine ills. Rizal rejected this alternative unless the people were prepared, morally and culturally, to build a free nation: 'Why independence if the slaves of today will be the tyrants of tomorrow?'

Rizal's activities stirred the powerful Spanish clergy and both his books were banned, the Dominicans charging that 'The work *Noli Me Tangere* has been found heretical, impious and scandalous from the religious perspective, anti-patriotic and subversive from the political point of view, injurious to the Spanish government ...'. While forming a non-violent organization called La Liga Filipina, Rizal was arrested and deported to Dapitan in Zamboanga.

During his four-year stay in Dapitan, Rizal set up a school in the Aristotelian manner, opened a hospital, installed a street lighting system from money won in a lottery, built a drainage system, introduced fishing methods, organized a cooperative to break the economic grip of the local Chinese merchant, wrote poems and carved sculpture. Through a secret emissary, the revolutionary organization, Katipunan, sought his involvement but he begged off, arguing that there were not enough guns to win. Instead he volunteered to serve as a medic in the Spanish Cuban war. He departed from Dapitan, unaware he was to die.

The Katipunan was uncovered. In the wake of night arrests, the leaders started the uprising. Although aboard a ship on the way to Cuba, Rizal was implicated, returned to Manila, tried, convicted, and publicly executed in Bagumbayan.

On his last night, he wrote a farewell poem which he concealed inside an alcohol lamp that he gave to his sister. *Ultimo Adios* is the best loved Filipino poem. Every Filipino knows at least the first lines '*Adios patria adorada …*'. At 35, an eye surgeon, scholar, linguist, painter and sculptor, musician and composer, novelist, certainly a young man of great promise for the race, was martyred, a victim of the filicidal nature of colonialism. No other Filipino claims as much respect and affection for his selfless exemplary life.

Austin Coates sums it up: 'In the history of the Philippines his life is an inescapable moment, a quintessence, a point of national identification—and a challenge to all who seek to emulate him.'

## Armed Struggle

Armed struggle (1896–1913) followed the Spanish colonial epoch. As Rizal had incisively assessed, the Katipunan did not have the military organization and power to defeat the Spaniards. The Supremo of the secret society, Andres Bonifacio, fell from power in a factional war, a victim of that old Filipino divisiveness. General Emilio Aguinaldo rose to power but at the expense of the military execution of Bonifacio, the first leader to be devoured by the Philippine revolution. At this stage of impasse, with the protagonists locked in negotiations and manoeuvres for control, the United States intervened under the gospel of 'manifest destiny'.

The Philippines was a key part of the Spanish-American war that was America's debut as a colonial power. Aguinaldo had been exiled to Hong Kong as part of the terms of an uneasy truce between the revolutionary forces and the Spanish in the Philippines. Working with the American Consul in Hong Kong, Rousenville Wildman,

Aguinaldo returned with guns, sailing with US Admiral Dewey who had destroyed the Spanish armada in Manila Bay.

The revolution revived, Aguinaldo marched towards Manila, apparently unaware of any American colonial designs on the Philippines. Yankee troops began to pour in while Aguinaldo battled the Spanish colonial forces until he threatened Manila. At this point, American troops were deployed, occupying strategic positions. The Spanish government in Manila surrendered to the Americans in a pre-arranged mock battle rather than face the wrath of Filipino rebels. The Spanish commander was subsequently court-martialled in Spain for his participation in the charade. The Americans had assured their occupation of Manila, and before long an incident in which American sentinels shot a Filipino revolutionary soldier swung the armed struggle from one against a 400-year-old colonizer to that against a brand new one.

The Americans refer to the subsequent battles as a 'Philippine insurrection', euphemism for a brutal war more widespread than the Filipino revolution against Spain. American military records list a body count of 16,000 *insurrectos* killed, 200,000 civilians dead. The US Army applied tactics used in the Indian wars, introducing a system of 'zoning' in which civilians were herded and confined to an area, those outside the parameters considered enemies to be shot.

Despite the capture of General Aguinaldo, the leader of the revolution, the conflict continued, outgunned Filipinos desperately switching to guerrilla warfare. In one incident in Samar, US marines, veterans of the Boxer rebellion in China, were annihilated in a well-planned guerrilla attack using mere *bolos*, provoking the US military to retaliate with a scorched-earth policy. 'I wish you to burn and kill, the more you burn and the more you kill, the better it will please me,' ordered Brigadier General Jacob H. Smith, who in his own words wanted Samar reduced to a 'howling wilderness'.

The Americans referred to the Filipinos as 'Goo-goos' and niggers. A song still lingers in the history of that war:

Damn Damn Damn the Filipino
Pockmarked Khadiak ladrone!
Underneath the starry flag
Civilize him with a Krag
And return us to our beloved home.

Military conquest did not end with the defeat of the Philippine revolutionary forces; the Muslims in southern Philippines continued armed resistance. The American military developed the .45 calibre bullet to knock down charging Moros who would not be felled by ordinary rifle bullets. The Moros were subjugated only in 1913.

Even after the armed struggle, the awakened nationalistic aspirations of Filipinos surfaced in other forms. Filipino playwrights used the Spanish *zarzuela* to present musical plays so intensely nationalistic in sentiment (the public would stand and cheer in response to covert symbols of the nation in bondage) that the Americans were forced to raid these theatrical houses and jail the playwrights of what they termed 'seditious plays'.

## The American Period

The bitter violence of the armed struggle left the vanquished Filipinos only with a desire for peace, and here the Americans redeemed themselves. The United States immediately introduced civil rights.

Cholera, dysentery, typhoid and smallpox had ravaged the populace constantly. Wartime conditions brought epidemics to frightening proportions and the Americans systematically imposed public sanitation that fathered the modern public health system. A public school system was set up, and volunteer American teachers arrived to teach the three R's, establishing English as the medium of instruction.

American-style journalism stirred notions of a free press. A political system was slowly introduced, with many of the young leaders handpicked by American administrators. In less than 40 years, a generation of Filipinos had emerged speaking English and

163

craving more Americanization. There were Filipino short story writers in English in the 1920s and by World War II a Filipino (Carlos Romulo) had won a Pulitzer prize.

The American-trained, English-speaking generation no longer communicated with the earlier Spanish *illustrado* generation. A serious generation gap was created. Fathers begot children who no longer knew, or cared, about the armed struggle. Filipino writers in Spanish had amassed a cultural legacy over centuries they could not hand down to a subsequent generation.

Aguinaldo's aide, General Artemio Ricarte, who never surrendered to the Americans, preferring self-exile in Japan instead, returned with Japanese forces in World War II only to find the new American-trained generation of Filipinos aligned with the Americans and angrily resisting the Japanese. Ricarte found himself cast in the light of a traitor when he had expected to return as liberator.

The American period (1900–1941) had culturally cut down an entire generation of Filipino *illustrados* in full flower. American tutelage brought forth children with no fathers. This *illustrado* generation retreated into the shadows of colonial houses, fading away with time, their ideas and manners ignored and forgotten by an exuberant generation in love with America, who could neither read nor speak the Spanish language of their parents.

## World War II: Japanese Influence

Lasting only three years, the World War II Japanese occupation of the Philippines affected Filipino attitudes because the Japanese, shocked at the Americanization of the society, sought to reawaken Asian roots. They made official a national language based on Tagalog. Moreover, the initial Japanese military victory proved the military vulnerability of America. Worse, it rudely demonstrated American interest in the Philippines was not the absolute commitment that Filipino kinship ways viewed it to be. Nationalism was reawakened.

On their return in 1945, the Americans recognized the independence of the Philippines, but never fully let go. Americans were granted equal parity rights in the newly forged Philippine constitution, US military bases enjoyed a 99-year lease with the right to interfere in any situation that involved national security.

When the Americans returned as liberators they were gratefully welcomed by the population who had been maltreated by the Japanese. Taking up where they had left off, American administrators handpicked leaders to run the country. General MacArthur chose a former brigadier-general on his staff, Manuel Roxas, who unfortunately had also served with the Japanese occupational government, thus tainting him with collaboration. The wartime collaboration issue was swept under the rug when Roxas won the election and became the first president of the newly independent republic.

The United States also provided 'backpay' for recognized guerrillas, a bonanza that regretfully failed to distinguish genuine patriots from opportunists. The postwar years were marked by a mixing up of heroes and heels, patriots and collaborators. To complicate matters, a resistance movement with communist ideology had gained a foothold during the war and the Americans worked to purge them. Pushed underground, the movement persists today as a pervasive armed network, evolving into the New People's Army.

## Postwar Republican Government

The postwar years were filled with cynicism and disillusionment. A republican form of government introduced a two-party system of free elections, patterned after the American model. But Filipino kinship values and group rivalry, rather than political ideas, determined the voting process. Patronage and *utang na loob* decided leadership and votes much more than political beliefs.

Mass media was one area relatively open for public expression of grievances and aspirations, and soon enough the youth, workers, women, everyone with an axe to grind, used the politics of the streets. At this point (1972), President Marcos declared martial law, dismantled the legislature, closed down all mass media, and imposed his own brand of government.

The Ferdinand and Imelda Marcos dictatorship proved to be a total disaster. Despite, or because of, full backing from the United States, the economy went into a tailspin, human rights were violently trampled upon, communist insurgency became a serious threat, and a Muslim separatist movement grew; all these while a select coterie of Marcos cronies amassed mega-fortunes.

Growing public dissatisfaction, coupled with knowledge that a terminally ill Marcos was moving towards dynastic succession, led to an aborted military coup, and this precipitated an incident which has become known as 'people power.' Hundreds of thousands of citizens, mostly the middle-class and disgruntled elite, gathered before the military camp where coup leaders had barricaded themselves to fend off the militia sent to squash the military rebels.

In a shining chapter in Philippine history, men and women, old and young, armed with only flowers and rosaries, faced down armoured military vehicles and battle-ready marines. The incident at the thoroughfare called EDSA caused the fall of Marcos, who fled with his family to American soil. A non-violent solution to topple a dictatorship had been spontaneously devised.

Corazon Aquino assumed office and restored pre-martial law institutions such as the Congress and the Senate, but to the disappointment of idealists, failed to turn the economy around or to stop the moral rot in Philippine society. Nevertheless, a democratic system of elections had been restored by Aquino and through this process the nation has sought to shape its future. Aquino's parting political act was to endorse the presidential candidacy of her Defence Minister, General Fidel Ramos, one of the chief architects of the Marcos martial law regime.

Fidel Ramos was sworn into office, after winning the 1992 elections. The new president worked towards reversing the economic slide throughout his six-year term. His successor, Joseph Estrada had hardly warmed his seat, after a landslide win in 1998, when scandals involving massive corruption and a growing harem of mistresses precipitated much vocal protest provoking Congress to initiate impeachment proceedings. The public participated in the drama first as spectators of the televised hearings, then taking to the streets spontaneously when eleven senators steamrolled a ruling not to allow vital bank documents as evidence and defections and resignations from Cabinet ministers and other key officials snowballed. Within three days, all the chiefs of the Armed Forces had taken the side of the populace, forcing Estrada to vacate his office after serving only 31 months. At noon on January 20, two hours before Estrada left the Palace in disgrace, Vice President Gloria Macapagal Arroyo was sworn in.

Nevertheless business remains somewhat stagnant as Estrada and post-martial law style politics has thrown the traffic of national programmes in a political gridlock. Over a million Filipinos have temporarily flown the coop, seeking economic relief all over the world: in nearby Hongkong and Singapore where many work as domestics, in far-off Saudi Arabia where they labour as construction workers; and in Europe where all passing Filipinos are now eyed suspiciously by officials as illegal migrants trying to sneak in to become household servants. It is the money they remit home to their families that keeps the balance of payments stable and miraculously saves the Philippine economy from collapse. The nation has yet to undergo a genuine epiphany, some visible sign of reform and change, a clear direction towards some positive goal. The legal and social machinery are in place but what remains missing is a national will. Perhaps the success of 'people power' this second time will bring greater civic awareness among leaders as well as with the vast but marginalized critical mass.

The legacy of World War II and the first four decades of the postwar years has been one of violence, graft and corruption, cynicism and pragmatism, creating a consumer society with little ideology. The Philippines never escaped the conditions of that world holocaust. Wrote Nick Joaquin: "At decades' end, when other countries had already smoothed away the scabs and scars of war, the Philippines was still in the same condition in which it had been left after the Japs and the GIs were through with it. And the makeshift devices of 'Liberation' days (the *barong-barong*, the jeepney, the

167

pontoon bridge, the Quonset hut office and theatre) had not been swept away in a general return to normal conditions of living but had, rather, become the norm. There was no return to 'normalcy,' for the simple reason that abnormality had become the Philippine way of life."

## The Filipino: Product of History

History shapes the character of a nation. The rich heritage of Filipinos demonstrates resilience and positive qualities that leave no doubt the Filipino people will overcome and prevail in the long haul. Meanwhile, in the short-term, history may serve to explain something of the present confusion of values. The ugly side of the Philippines a foreigner encounters today was shaped over two colonial periods when the society's indigenously emerging messiahs—a natural crop of idealistic leaders—were brutalized for pragmatic colonial ends.

Filipinos today are often at loggerheads over what values and virtues, and manners and etiquette, should apply. Scholars and artists are searching the past, the nooks and crannies of the archipelago—and their own souls—for the Filipino identity. One can proudly point to a good number of beautiful things.

Filipinos have begun to shape their own destiny in the new millennium. In 1986, 'people power' was invented to peacefully depose a tyrant. This right is now enshrined in the new Constitution. There are overtones of the Filipino fiesta in these 'people power' events. In the most recent resort to 'people power,' the military played only a subdued role, and the United States, unlike in the ousting of Marcos, none at all. A Filipino-style democracy is evolving, in which good can make a difference in the dominant politics of kinship and plunder.

Whenever an unpleasant side puts foreigners in a state of culture shock, they should try to see this present period as a transitional phase: Filipinos trying to make sense out of the savage intrusion of diverse cultures, and the violence of armed struggle from which the nation never fully recovered.

# Chapter Eight

# THE LIFE CIRCLE

*Item:* A blonde, blue-eyed American visiting a *barrio* finds himself the focus of attention of pregnant women, some of them touching him and giggling. It doesn't mean he is a sex symbol; neither is he being ridiculed. Filipinos believe that the physical qualities of a child in a womb can be influenced by the mother's peculiar prenatal cravings and obsessions. Many desire for their child a fair skin.

*Item:* A Filipino friend suffers a death in his family and you come to commiserate. At the wake you find the room a bustle with food being served and others noisily playing card games. It is not

169

callous disrespect for the departed relative, nor a surprise party; they are the side effects of any gathering of the kin. This boisterous emotional support is seen as a way to commiserate with the surviving kin by keeping their spirits up.

## Shaping the Child from the Womb

Rites of passage for Filipinos are a blend of Western influences and traditional kinship ways. A child's existence begins with *lihi*, a reference to the peculiar cravings a pregnant woman develops. She may suddenly express a strong irrational urge to eat green mangoes in the middle of the night; a loving husband is supposed to cater to her whim and brave the typhoon rains in search of his loved one's momentary object of desire. It is popularly believed that physical qualities of the object of obsession rub off on the features and temperament of the child.

In rural Philippines, when the child is born the placenta is buried in the ground underneath the house; but in the cities attention is on health procedures for the newborn infant. Baptism is considered the first rite of passage; the child becomes Catholic, is formally christened with a name, and acquires a *ninong* and a *ninang* (godparents).

From the time of conception through birth and early infancy, therefore, parents of Filipino children try to influence their character and temperament. The father's indulgence of his pregnant wife's extraordinary fixations reflects a fatherly concern, since these cravings are believed to influence the baby in the womb. The mother's *lihi* could also express itself in strange aversions, even to her own husband, and this too is believed to influence the child's personality. Would-be mothers who become irritable with their husbands and develop phobias for their husband's mannerisms during pregnancy, are said to give birth to children exactly like their fathers.

Post-birth beliefs and practices, such as the burying of the placenta or the secreting away in roof beams of the umbilical cord, are also designed to influence the child's future; a placenta thrown into the stream will make the child a wanderer. A newspaper and a pencil buried with it will make the child intelligent. Finally, at the first formal rite of passage, baptism, the parents carefully select the godparents, because a life-long bond is expected to be established between child and godparents. (See chapter 3, pages 48–51.)

## One of a Crowd

In rural areas, children are born at home with all the family fully aware of the event. They are cared for not just by the mother, but by the father, grandparents, uncles and aunts, and if they have older brothers or sisters, by them too. They grow up learning to care for those younger than themselves. The result is a total awareness of self in relation to a constellation of other people.

Guthrie and Jimenez-Jacobs' study, *Child Rearing and Personality Development in the Philippines*, makes this point: 'The Filipino child is never alone. In a one-room house with many siblings and other relatives the child may be several years old before he has his

*Families this size live together, often in cramped homes.*

171

first experience of being out of sight of others. In addition, he is carried, handled, and touched a great deal, and, of course, he may possibly never sleep alone throughout his whole life span. Since he is in such continuing contact with others, he develops a good many techniques for handling the variety of stresses which inevitably arise. With the fundamental importance to him of activities in this domain, his personality in formation and structure is oriented to his relationships with others.'

## The American Child in Contrast

Cultural differences with Western lifestyles have their roots here. Guthrie draws the contrast with the American child who is 'most frequently born in an impersonal environment removed from the home with relatives and siblings excluded'; also, in the first days, only the nuclear family sees the American child; feeding and toilet training are deemed the mother's responsibility.

'An American mother does not as a rule share her child-rearing duties with relatives or at times even with her husband.' This maternal source of attention, Guthrie believes, could be the cause of sibling rivalry in American families since no other adults attend the child and the mother '... alone offers predictable attention or displeasures'.

The American child is brought up to be independent, the pioneer who did what everybody said could not be done. Hostilities are acceptable and manageable within the small nuclear American family and thus allowed play. The child is encouraged to express itself, even if it means losing points with neighbours and friends. It is directed towards its own age group and has little interaction with older or younger people. It must develop its own interests and use its own resources, seeking family support only as a last resort.

## Filipino Teasing as Control

Filipino children are controlled through teasing. They learn to cope with limitations and inadequacies brought out in the form of teasing from elders and other children; similarly, they are able to express objections or defend interests, disguising aggression or disrespect on the grounds they are only teasing. Teasing keeps children in line, making them sensitive to self-esteem, and thereby building awareness of *hiya* and *amor-propio*. Teasing remains throughout life a basic tool for otherwise unacceptable expressions, for control, and for 'feeling out' another's reactions. Teasing reveals children's or parents' attitudes and views without openly discussing sensitive issues such as grooming habits, school marks, choice of sweetheart, greed, laziness, and so on.

Within the closed universe of the kinship group, children are not taught to fend for themselves and develop their own resources; rather they are encouraged to consider every family member in whatever they do. Interdependence is the rhythm of their life. The unending theme Filipino children hear is: 'If you have your needs others also have theirs and they merit equal importance.' The bigger the family and kin group the more conflict of wants, and the more children must accommodate. They are often asked to yield in the same way that others, too, have on occasion to yield to them. They develop extrasensory perceptions of moods and unspoken opinions.

For children, there is little distinction between the sexes. Unlike English where the pronoun 'she' or 'he' distinguishes the sexes, Tagalog uses a sexless pronoun. Since Filipino families are bilateral, the mother's kin enjoy equal importance. Women in the Philippines, in general, reach many positions of wealth and power.

Sexual curiosity at an early age is brushed aside by telling the child it is too young, but children are not filled with notions that sex is wrong. They slowly tend to play games associated with their sex.

## Circumcision

On reaching puberty, the boy starts to wear long pants and he is usually circumcised. This is not a ceremony that involves the family. The boy goes with his friends to someone in the *barrio* or neighbourhood who is known to do the job—often the town barber. It is performed in private, with a razor or sharp *bolo*. The boy applies boiled guava leaves on the wound to help speed the healing. By word of mouth, older family members learn of the circumcision, but not much is openly said about it. In major cities, doctors perform the operation in a hospital, at birth or a few days later.

The rite makes the boy a man. He learns about sex through his peers. Circumcision has no religious significance, neither is it a family ritual. In fact, it is considered a personal choice of the boy, and from this point he expands his family ties with male companions of his age. It is more a macho act. Filipinos question derisively the manhood of someone who has not been circumcised with the derogatory term *supot*.

## Female Adolescence

The female child reaches puberty with menstruation, which is not marked with any ceremony. She is counselled by her mother and elder sisters, mostly on hygiene. Through teasing, she is taught feminine behaviour and modesty—keeping her legs together when seated, for example. She may be selected as a *reina* in a Flores de Mayo affair, grooming her for a role in society where beauty and grace are valued. 'Dressing up' and learning beauty techniques are her preoccupations.

## Growing Up in the Philippines

Very little, if any, sex education is given by parents. Young people have to fend for themselves by jokes and conversations with their peers. Acquiring sexual education by sharing information on sex, courtship styles and romantic gossip, the young male (*binata*) and female (*dalaga*) extend their kin group world to friends of the same age and the same sex. In cities the young person's gang-mates are called *barkada*. The young fraternize with their *barkada* and other *barkadas* until they marry.

Education provides a different world for children, who learn things their parents may have little familiarity with. It is regarded as a chance for upward mobility, a better lifestyle. School is a world outside the kin group, and children make their own friends.

There are some minor milestones. A child's First Communion is important, so too the religious ceremony of Confirmation, where again godparents are involved. Graduation in elementary, secondary and tertiary levels of education is celebrated. Some complain of the excessive costs such ceremonies involve; others want bigger ceremonies and even one for kindergarten graduation.

As young girls blossom, they aspire to be popular with boys, to be selected for Muse in the class, beauty queen of a social club or during school balls; men strive to be macho with their gang-mates and popular with the ladies. Boys and girls get to know each other and engage in informal courtship in groups during social gatherings. Dating is generally in foursomes or more, rarely a one-on-one affair.

## Debut Etiquette

Among the wealthy, when a girl turns 18 she is deemed ready for marriage and is formally presented to society with a social dance called a debut, a big affair to which relatives and friends of both the girl and her parents are invited. As dancing is popular among Filipinos, countless hours are spent practising for these social gatherings. For weeks, a group of the celebrant's close friends rehearse the *cotillon*. It is an honour to be chosen to dance in the *cotillon*.

The debut dinner is usually catered and guests are assigned to tables. The kin and their prominent friends are assigned a group of tables and the young unmarrieds another group of tables.

Single young people are invited with their dates. Among the young group, the male guest picks up his date at her home and gives her a corsage. The celebrant and her father open the dance with a waltz, after which the rest of the guests may join in. Dress on this occasion is formal.

*In social circumstances, such as the* sunduan, *young people get to know each other in the public eye, their romantic aspirations part of the community's awareness.*

## *Getting Married to a Filipina*

Marriage is a personal choice of the girl and boy, but because of strong kinship ties, their immediate family often tries to have a say. It is customary for the boy to obtain the girl's parents' approval even before he actually begins formal courtship, which is viewed as 'house-calling' (*umaakyat ng bahay*). Romance outside this framework is conceded, but many prefer the conventional system which allows strong family participation. This is because in a Filipino marriage more than a boy and a girl are joined in a bond; families of both sides develop ties, especially once a child is born; and the *compadrazco* ceremony further cements both families by ritual.

*A suitor and his friends are received by his girl's family.*

When a boy has proposed and a girl has accepted, he formally asks for her hand, a ritual requiring the parents of the boy (or if an orphan, the elder brother or a prominent acquaintance) to pay a call on the girl's parents. The couple merely sits and listens.

Wedding plans are discussed, a delicate matter since both families are involved up to their ears, and may have entirely different notions of how the wedding should be celebrated. How much the wishes of the two sweethearts are entertained at all depends on the graciousness of their parents. Wedding expenses are shouldered by the groom's parents, therefore their ideas have to be taken seriously, along with their means to provide a feast. The number of guests is agreed upon, the venue, the sponsors, etc., with the couple expressing their preferences. It is important that both families get off to a good start.

Among the upper and middle classes the prospective groom gives the girl a ring, and you can be sure the size and quality of the stone become a subject of talk. This marks the couple's formal engagement, a period that could last several days or much longer. The girl's family gives a dinner called *despedida de soltera* (farewell to maidenhood), and her friends hold a bridal shower; the former is borrowed from Spanish custom, the latter from the Americans. The *despedida de soltera* is the occasion for the couple's families to get to know each other. The bridal shower is a female affair with the bride's friends bringing something for the future bride's use: kitchen utensils, etc. When the bride has her first baby, they may fete her with a baby shower, offering her things for the new baby.

If a couple marries against family wishes, they elope, an accepted practice in which they run off to marry, and stay with a sympathetic relative or friend. The parents' usual reaction is withdrawal of support. Neutral parties (brothers, aunts, uncles and old friends) then try to act as go-betweens to get the parents to forgive and forget. If they will not be reconciled, the couple will visit them with their firstborn to formally seek forgiveness and reunion. The parents' anger melts at the sight of their grandchild, and soon all is well.

## Married Life

It is still customary for newlyweds to live with the boy's or the girl's parents, at least for a year until they settle down. Breaking off from the parents can provoke an emotional crisis because Filipino parents are reluctant to let go. Parents regard the desire of their married children to live on their own as caused by unhappiness and a failure of harmony within the kin group home. (This is also true of bachelors who desire to live on their own, a most unheard of practice in the past; the family fears the community will interpret such a move as the result of a disagreement in the family, and of course *hiya* will not permit such an impression, even if true.) In Manila, the system of having married children live in separate houses within a common area called a compound shows family togetherness.

Ultimately, however, the young couple get off on their own. Moving into a new house signals an important beginning. The new homeowners may hold a house-blessing or housewarming party.

## House-Blessing Ritual

When Filipinos move into a new house they have a house-blessing. They believe it is not proper to live in a house unless it is blessed in the presence of friends who will wish them prosperity. Friends and relatives are invited. There is a religious ritual where prayers are said and a priest sprinkles holy water in every corner of the house. Important guests hold candles which are provided by the host. Sometimes an elder guest will throw a shower of coins for good luck. After the blessing there is a feast.

Where the house has been specially built for the new homeowners, silver coins will be placed in the major posts before construction begins, and they check that the number of steps of main stairways is not divisible by three. The owner counts the steps, '*oro, plata, mata, oro, plata, mata* (gold, silver, death)'; a bad omen, if it ends in *mata*.

In rural areas the first object that must be brought into a new house is a pot of rice. All these beliefs revolve on hopes for prosperity associated with the young couple establishing their own nuclear family in their own house.

Guests are not expected to bring anything—just a hearty appetite. Close friends may bring a small item for the house, but this is not expected. In some cases an image of the sacred heart or the family patron saint is enshrined.

## The Blessing of Children

Children are considered God's blessing on the marriage. Childless couples are looked upon with much sympathy by Filipinos who are never lacking in advice on how to have children. They will cite personal cases of successful formerly-childless couples, offer medical theories and names of noted specialists, or suggest religious novenas to special saints, and even dancing at the fiesta of Obando, where an ancient fertility dance before San Pascual Baylon persists.

The role of mother is regarded as the most fulfilling role of the Filipina. It is at this stage that the Filipino life cycle becomes matriarchal. Children are regarded as the binding force keeping the family together. The mother assumes supervision of the children as well as the administration of the household. She mothers her husband and holds the purse strings. The male is expected only to be a breadwinner, a role outside the home; and at this point the male may start to stray. Filipino standards tend to tolerate extramarital activities of the husband while frowning very severely upon any sign of infidelity by the wife. She is, after all, the symbol of motherhood.

## No Success Without Kin Group Acceptance

A new nuclear family strives for material security and the approval of the community. The wife is often free to develop her own enterprising nature, and she is always regarded as an important supplementary earner. Material prosperity and professional success are evaluated in terms of the accompanying esteem of the community, otherwise any such advancement is viewed as incomplete. Thus the nuclear family seeks to share any success or pleasure through feasts, inviting kin and all important people and friends. A job promotion, winning the lottery, a distinguished professional award, winning a beauty contest; all these are occasions for a 'blowout', a treat, sharing the family honour and the lucky moment.

Other occasions for festivities are birthdays (key milestones are the 40th and 50th) and wedding anniversaries, with special significance for the 1st, 10th, 20th, 25th (silver anniversary), 50th (golden anniversary), and 60th (diamond anniversary). A renewal of vows is a popular way to celebrate silver or golden wedding anniversaries.

## Growing Old

Middle and old age are lived in the warmth and security of a three to four-generation family complex, from the homeowner's parents to his own children and grandchildren. Homes for the elderly do not exist in the Philippines; children consider it a sacred obligation to care for their parents in their old age. Elderly people never lose their place of respect and affection, and grandchildren often go to them for personal counsel.

## The Filipino Way to Go

Just as occasions such as anniversaries, school graduations and baptisms, gather the family together, so do times of crisis, such as illness, hospitalization and death.

'Rites of passage' end in Christian burial in the town cemetery. These days 'memorial parks' have grown in popularity, logical offshoots of Filipino funeral rites. The American 'Forest Lawn' style with well-trimmed lawns and ground-level markers just did not suit Filipino notions of grave markers; above-ground ones, the bigger the better, as well as family mausoleums to house remains and visitors, are preferred.

Filipinos come to commiserate immediately upon learning of the death of a relative or friend. The family stands vigil over the corpse day and night, taking turns, until burial which could be as long as three days later. The widow or widower, children and close family members receive guests who come to pay their last respects and console the bereaved. It is customary to send flowers, or a Mass card offering prayers. In instances where the family is known to be in economic difficulty, money is donated to help with the burial expenses (*abuloy*).

Because all the kin are expected to come, refreshments are always ready. Food is an important social element and hospitality demands the offering of some food or drink to any visitor, even if one is mourning the loss of mother, husband, or some close relative.

## *Mourning*

A Filipino wake is anything but solemn, but Filipinos try to maintain a less boisterous air than normal, and a sense of loss is the spirit of the occasion. Immediate family members wear black, the widow and the other women donning black veils. Men wear dark trousers and a white shirt with a black armband. Traditionally, mourning clothes were worn for a year, at which time a ceremony marking the first anniversary of the death signified when mourning clothes were shed (*babang luksa*) and the immediate family could return to normal colourful attire.

These days there is a more lax attitude regarding mourning attire. But the community would still frown on a widow shedding her black after only a day of mourning; a decent period is still expected to be allowed to pass before life returns to normal. A novena or nine days of prayer (usually with a Mass), is held after the burial and this is now considered the occasion to end the period of mourning.

Visitors register their name and address at the wake, and the bereaved family sends a prayer card and thanks after the period of mourning. It is also customary for the well-off to place an obituary in the newspapers announcing the death and the time and place of the burial rites. This obituary also lists the names of the immediate family and great care is taken that no name is overlooked. After the burial, a notice of thanks is also published in the newspapers.

Among rural folk, the traditional wake is occasion for poetical jousts or parlour-game riddles to keep those holding vigil awake.

## *Funeral Etiquette*

1. The deceased's family publishes an obituary stating the time and place of the funeral and the names of the family members.
2. Send flowers or a Mass card (handed to the closest kin present). The obituary may carry a note to omit flowers. Check for this.
3. Sign a book placed near the entrance of the funeral parlour. Add your address so it is convenient to send you a thank you card.
4. Express condolences to the widow or widower and the children (distinguished by their black). A 15 to 30-minute stay is enough.
5. You may be offered food and drink. You need not take either.
6. Friends may gather outside the church or funeral parlour and reminisce about the deceased.
7. It is not necessary to go to both the wake and the funeral unless you were close to the deceased.
8. It is often customary to donate some money to the family if the deceased was not well-off (this gift is called *abuloy*).
9. Thank you cards are sent to those who attended the wake and the funeral.
10. Black or dark sombre colours are worn to the wake. White is also acceptable. Close kin are expected to wear black and white.

Nine days of Mass and religious services are held after the burial. Close kin and friends attend these. On the ninth day food and drinks are served to thank those who have come to commiserate, for helping the family during the vigil. Mourning clothes are shed on this day (traditionally this was done on the first anniversary of the death). As a sign of mourning, a piece of black ribbon or a rectangular black pin is worn by mourners.

## Remembering Departed Kin

Death rituals do not end with burial and the mourning period. Filipinos commemorate a death anniversary, holding Mass or visiting graves and inviting relatives and friends to a reunion. 'In memoriam' notices are published in newspapers by wealthy families on death anniversaries. The memory of prominent people who have had the support of the well-to-do is formally perpetuated through a group organized around the immediate family under the title 'friends of…'; it holds a ceremony on his birthday or death anniversary.

## Days for the Dead

On All Saints Day (November 1) and All Souls Day, which follows, the dead are honoured. Filipinos flock to cemeteries to clean or whitewash gravestones, tidy plots and pay respects to departed kin as a family group. Poorly maintained graves reflect the kin's lack of regard for the dead. Many hold an all-night vigil and light candles over tombstones.

In typical fiesta spirit, entrepreneurs have cashed in on the huge throngs at the cemeteries to hawk candles, flowers, refreshments, and toys. To the cemeteries on All Saints and All Souls Days come relatives of the dead, including children. They may have a brief prayer ceremony (a priest gives blessings), then begin chatting, and soon enough refreshments materialize. Families have been known to roast a whole pig at the gravesite, bring tables and chairs for mahjong during night vigil, and even transistor radios and a portable TV (perched on the gravestone), to while away vigil hours. Some mausoleums have beds. One in Parañaque has a helipad, in case one decides to visit by helicopter! It's the Filipino way of death.

## All Saints Day Etiquette

1. Dress is expected to be sombre and sedate.
2. Religious rites for the dead are performed by a priest over the grave marker.

3. Relatives may reflect or say prayers over the grave, standing vigil over the grave marker for about half an hour.
4. Candles may be lit and placed on top of the tomb.
5. A vase of flowers or a simple bouquet is an appropriate gesture.

*On All Souls Day, young ones in the barrios serenade neighbours who offer money or ginger tea. Youths play pranks or steal chickens after their rounds, all in the spirit of fun.*

# Chapter Nine

# PROFILE OF A FILIPINO

"She's shy, demure, modest, and loyal.
And boy, is she *ever* self-effacing!" sea.

## FILIPINO WOMEN

In *A Study of Psychopathology*, Filipino psychiatrist Lourdes V.
Lapus writes: 'The Filipino culture, for all the increasing signs and
protests to the contrary, still has a large hangover from its ego-ideal
for women of many bygone years. This is the so-called "Maria
Clara" image of a woman who is shy, demure, modest, self-effacing,
and loyal to the end. The openly provocative, sexually aggressive
female who is frequently associated with the American female
image is still comparatively rare in the Filipino culture ...'

Filipinas generally strive to portray the 'Maria Clara' image and frown on aggressive displays by women. An aggressive woman, which description includes one who is open and mixes freely with men, is considered sexually 'loose'. Cultural norms favour the demure, modest female when it comes to personal, social or business relationships with men. Social inferiority is not implied. The Filipina enjoys equality with men in many areas, notably in professional, business and career areas.

To understand the Filipina, one must look at the different roles she takes in society. As she goes through life, the Filipina may take the roles of daughter, sister, *dalaga* or young woman, wife, mother, mistress, professional, employer, employee, etc. The first few roles will be discussed in more detail as they are more firmly entrenched in tradition and probably influence the more modern roles that a Filipina faces.

## *The Daughter*

Due to the importance of the family in Filipino culture, it is impressed on every individual from childhood that parents are owed a debt of gratitude for bringing one into this world. (This is balanced by the belief and tradition that parents should make sacrifices for their children because they brought them into the world.) Obedience to parents and to older siblings is taught early and enforced until adulthood, whereupon it becomes one's sense of obligation.

Children never attain equal footing with parents; parents are always treated with respect and the debt of gratitude is a lifetime one. Children are expected to serve their parents until their death. Through this system the older citizens are provided and cared for. There is no need for nursing homes or homes for the aged. In fact, putting one's parents in such a home would reflect badly on the individual and incur *hiya*. One would be labelled a bad son or daughter who does not love one's parents—probably the greatest sin in the eyes of Philippine society.

For the Filipino daughter, mother serves as the first model. She has a great impact in a society where role modelling is the main process operating in the learning of sex roles. This factor together with the cultural dynamics described above, plus the prolonged physical and emotional nurture received from the mother, creates a special bond between mother and daughter.

Greater service is usually expected from the daughter than from the son when it comes to satisfying a mother's needs. On the daughter's part, mother is the first person she turns to in times of trouble and she is the first source of knowledge on household and family matters.

## Ate: *The Sister*

Sisters play a very important role in Philippine families, especially older sisters. An older sister is called *Ate* by her siblings. *Ate* is responsible for the younger children and she may bathe, dress and feed them. This is necessary in large families where the mother cannot look after all the children. Older children are taught early that it is their duty to help take care of younger brothers and sisters. This provides them with training and experience in housewifely and motherly duties. The oldest girl assumes this role as soon as the second or third child comes along and not necessarily when she reaches a certain age. It is not uncommon to see a small child carrying a younger brother or sister who is more than half her size.

Her role of 'deputy mother' commands *Ate* the respect of her younger siblings who look to her for advice in personal matters. They are expected to obey her just as they do their mother, because she is there to look after their best interests. She may serve as an intermediary between them and their parents particularly in large families where some of the children are not as close to their parents or where parents are rather strict. In the event of the parents' death, it is she who takes over the responsibility of keeping the family together.

The name *Ate* is also used among cousins or same-generation kin in relationships which operate along the lines described above, a situation which is common in Filipino extended-kin systems.

## Dalaga: *The Young Woman*

The role of the *dalaga* or young woman, like other roles, is delineated by society. The code of ethics is learned via role modelling and by direct instructions from parents and teachers (e.g. young girls are often told 'girls should sit with their legs together'). Behaviour is controlled by teasing, by gossip and the fear of being the subject of malicious gossip.

Society expects a young woman to conduct herself with decorum and to appear modest and shy, especially among men. She should never flaunt her sexuality otherwise she will be labelled a 'flirt' and considered sexually 'loose'.

Perhaps the most complicated aspect of her role is the part she plays in courtship. Courtship in the Philippines is a game which both parties (young men and women) enjoy tremendously. The young lady is supposed to play 'hard to get'; she should not show too great an interest in a man, some even going to the point of pretending total disinterest. How hard a time she gives her suitor increases her worth in his and in others' eyes.

Young men go all out in courting a girl. They send her flowers, give her presents and ring her up every night. A young man's devotion is measured by such overtures. A girl does not usually say 'yes' to the first invitation from a new suitor. He may have to ask her several times before she agrees to go out with him. Her first few refusals are not taken as rejections but rather interpreted to mean she is playing hard to get. The disadvantage of this system is that a real rejection may not be detected and some men are very persistent!

The men try to outdo each other in sweet talk or *bola* which may best be translated as 'bull'. Corny lines and clichés such as 'you are the only one in my life' and 'I dream of you every night' flow freely.

189

Since these lines are used on many different girls they lose a bit of their sincerity and when a girl is taken in by them the young man boasts to his friends that she was *kagat na kagat* which, loosely translated, means 'she really bit into it'—i.e., she took the bait—hook, line and sinker.

This sometimes backfires on a young man when he meets a girl he really cares about who warily regards his now sincere remarks as merely *bola*. Young ladies are thus faced with the challenge of how to tell when a guy is 'making *bola*'. As with all boy-girl relationships, there are many who get hurt. But it's all a game and if you lose one round there's always a chance you'll win the next one.

## The Wife

The Filipino wife is a victim of double standards imposed by society. The responsibility of keeping a marriage together is usually placed on her so she does not get much sympathy if she complains of her husband's transgressions. A wife who complains openly or speaks ill of her husband is not respected by society because family failings are supposed to be kept within the family. To speak badly of your husband and broadcast his weaknesses is to degrade your own family, thus breaking the first rule in the Filipino code of ethics.

In Philippine society it is not uncommon for a man to have a mistress or mistresses—it is accepted and considered a symbol of masculinity. The wife is expected to tolerate this. Furthermore, she is often given the blame in such situations. One will hear people say 'It's probably because so-and-so doesn't fix herself properly or look after his needs', etc. It is the wife's responsibility to do something about it. Confronting the husband and/or his mistress is not very effective and does not get her much sympathy. The best strategy for her is to try to win him back by being attentive and looking her best for him. Using this strategy in earnest will also gain her the support and sympathy of the people around her. Once she obtains this, the battle is half won, for with the support of mutual friends and relatives, the husband may be pressured to give up his mistress or at least be more attentive to his wife.

A good wife by Filipino standards is one who looks after the best interests of her husband, who gives him emotional and perhaps material support and who manages the household and children efficiently. The husband does not usually concern himself with household matters and does not have much to do with the children until they are in their teens—whereupon he is called in to give a hand with discipline. There are no restrictions on wives working, as long as they do not neglect the duties outlined above. Most wives in Manila have some sort of business on the side and there are many who work as professionals.

The advantage of having servants to run the household is exploited to the fullest. This is one of the great attractions living in the Philippines provides women. The lifestyle offers many good opportunities for women to fulfill themselves. Dr Lapuz, in *Filipino Marriages in Crisis*, states: 'Despite her seemingly second-rate status in the marriage, the Filipino wife has a large sphere of influence. She is closer emotionally to the children than her husband is and she is intimately involved in their growth and development— for the longest time. In crucial areas of home life, e.g. child-rearing, breadwinning, and even in deciding the husband's choice of friends, she subtly or pointedly wields her influence. If her activities are understood as derived from wifely intentions to keep husband, home, and children in good condition, and to foster family advancement, she can do almost anything.'

## Querida: *The Mistress*

The role played by the mistress is essentially also that of wife and mother. In many cases the mistress is preferred over the wife because the former is a better wife to a man than the latter. There is usually much rivalry between her and the wife, not on bedroom matters, but on who cooks better and who takes better care of the husband.

The Filipino mistress is really more like a second wife and is regarded as such by her partner. Often she has children by him whom he supports and considers as important as his legitimate children. Many Filipinos have two or more families 'on the side' and it is a wonder how they manage to support them all. Of course these families are not recognized by the predominantly Catholic society but the mistress still considers herself as her partner's wife and claims rights over him which naturally gives rise to conflicts with the legitimate wife.

## The Mother

Children are of great importance in family-oriented Philippine culture. They form the link that binds the wife's family to the husband's. They also present opportunities for extending kin relations through the *compadrazco* system. Hence, Filipinas expect and are expected to have children once they marry.

The role of mother is probably the most important role a Filipina will assume in the course of her life. Since the mother is in charge of household matters and the responsibility of the children lies mainly with her, she is in a position of power. This power is not to be underestimated considering that kinship dynamics is the central propitiating force in Philippine society, as illustrated by the prevalence of nepotism in many areas.

Her power comes from the sense of obligation to parents instilled in children. There is also another factor that comes into it—the sense of belonging and ownership which characterizes Filipino relationships. In *A Study of Psychopathology*, Dr Lapuz states: 'A person grows up in the Filipino culture with one paramount assumption: that he belongs to someone. When he presents his self to others, it is with his family that he is identified. He belongs to the family as a whole as well as to its members.' She goes on to say: 'Between the parents, there is a further choice as to whom one belongs. Almost always, it is the mother. The loyalty, allegiance and sense of obligation are stronger with her than with father. One must never cause her hurt or displeasure. The greater attachment to the mother is, of course, inevitable not only because of biological circumstances, but also because of the prolonged intense emotional nurturing received from her. Here is where to belong gains the meaning of to be loved, cared for, and protected.'

This 'ownership' type of relationship gives the mother certain rights over the child. For example, she believes she has the right to know her children's private thoughts and thus encourages the confiding of problems and secrets. While she does this with the intention of guiding their thinking and advising them properly, there may also be an unconscious or perhaps subconscious wish to make them emotionally dependent on her, thus giving her a greater hold on them. A mother also has the right to advise her children who in turn are taught to take such advice meekly because it is given in their interest.

George M. Guthrie and Pepita Jimenez Jacobs did a cross-cultural study on child-rearing entitled *Child Rearing and Personality Development in the Philippines*. They compared their findings with those of Sears, Maccoby and Levin on the patterns of child-rearing among American mothers. Some of the more obvious and important differences they report are: Filipino mothers are more lenient and permissive about feeding intervals, weaning and toilet-training than their American counterparts; American mothers use denial of privileges, threats of loss of love, and physical punishment to enforce obedience, while Filipino mothers are more likely to punish physically, scold, or bribe; American mothers do not as a rule share their child-rearing duties with relatives whereas Filipino children are surrounded by many adults who share in the responsibility of their upbringing.

Some differences between the two cultures were attributed to environment but most appear to have stemmed from dissimilar cultural emphasis. For example, the child-rearing practices of Filipino mothers are directed and determined by the cultural emphasis on the importance of the family and smooth interpersonal relations. The difference in emphasis in Philippine and American cultures is expressed succinctly in the following statement by Guthrie and Jacobs: 'The Philippine ideal is not self-sufficiency and independence but rather family sufficiency and a refined sense of reciprocity.' This was demonstrated quite clearly in their study on Philippine parental attitudes towards their children. They make the following comment in their discussion of their findings: 'Parents do not express the hope that their children will be ambitious or show great achievements. There is no mention of a child becoming rich or famous. On the contrary, they stress the hope that their child will heed family values.'

Although the upbringing of Filipino children may be shared by others in the family, the main responsibility lies with the mother. While the others may play with them or help them dress, etc., it is the mother who disciplines them. Her role is acknowledged by society and consequently it is she who receives the credit when they grow up to be good members of the community, and the blame when they fail. Filipinos believe that children's behaviour reflects their parents' attitudes. Hence the mother places paramount importance on the task of instilling the cultural values of family sufficiency and *pakikisama*, the ability to get along smoothly with others.

The role of the mother does not end upon the marriage of her children. Although it is diminished, she still remains a powerful figure in the life of her children. She can influence major decisions regarding their lives and may even be involved in trivial ones such as choosing curtains for the kitchen or the baby's room. When grandchildren arrive she inevitably has to have a say in the baptismal celebrations or at least know everything concerning the child. This often gives rise to conflict between a wife and her mother-in-law, a situation not uncommon in Philippine society. In such situations the husband is always caught in the middle. He must never openly go against his mother because it is his duty first and foremost to be a good son. On the other hand he cannot ignore his wife's complaints and may often sympathize with her. Yet he is powerless to do anything and, although the wife complains to him and wants him to intervene, she knows he cannot and never will. She will also never openly defy or confront her mother-in-law.

There is usually a great effort on the wife's part to get along with her mother-in-law. In *Filipino Marriages in Crisis*, Dr Lapuz comments: 'It is a tribute, dubious perhaps, to the Filipino daughter-in-law that she continues to want to be liked by her husband's mother.' Part of the reason for this is the power the mother-in-law wields over her son. Good relations with the mother-in-law ensures support, both material and emotional, which naturally would make life easier for the wife/daughter-in-law. It is important to understand the unique position in which the Filipino daughter-in-law is placed in a situation which occurs across many different cultures. Because of it, she may not respond in the way her American or European counterparts would.

## Matandang Dalaga: *The spinster*

The Filipino spinster or *matandang dalaga* is not a liberated individual, free from responsibilities. Although she does not have her own family of procreation (husband and children), she is still tied to her family of orientation (parents, brothers and sisters, aunts, uncles, etc.), and she has duties and obligations to them. She may live with one of her brothers or sisters, serving them in the form of assisting in household management, or she may continue to live with her parents, serving them and looking after them in their old age. There is also a position set aside for her in her local church— she is in charge of its upkeep and maintenance. Hence she has a definite role in the family and in society. In this way she feels she 'belongs' to someone and her family keeps her from getting lonely.

There is some social stigma attached to spinsters, though. Because of the great emphasis and importance attached to getting married and having children, most Filipinos do not understand how a woman can be over 30 or 35 and still be unmarried. The only reason they can think of is that she did not receive any offers. Hence the *matandang dalaga* is seen as someone who was 'left on the shelf'.

Often the Filipina will be playing any number of the above roles at the same time and the ease with which she moves from one to the other as the situations for them arise is truly a skill she must be credited with. The key to it all is to always think 'Family First'.

One other role assumed by Filipino women is that of keeper of family virtues. Older Filipinas consider it their duty to keep the family's reputation in good stead and thus have no qualms about giving their opinions on what is right and wrong regarding behaviour, attitudes, quarrels and conflicts which concern or directly reflect on the family. Through them, deviant behaviour is controlled and curtailed via direct confrontations and/or intermediaries.

Finally, a note on the Filipina's remarkable skill as an entrepreneur. Almost every Filipino wife is involved in some business 'on the side'—whether it be a small store, a kiosk selling drinks and snacks, selling paintings through friends and contacts, a cake shop or perhaps accepting orders at home, selling boutique goods, etc.— and what's more, doing very well at it. Many big businesses are run by Filipino women. Filipinas figure prominently in the business world. To give some examples: the Philippine Women's University was founded by a Filipina and is still run efficiently by Filipinas; one of Makati's biggest and most popular department stores is owned and managed by a Filipina; the two biggest bookstore chains are owned and were built up by two Filipina sisters.

Aside from their ability in managing businesses, Filipinas can also be powerful figures in the background, holding true the saying 'Behind every great man is a woman'. In the case of the Filipino it is a wife or a mother. The Filipina is very adept at social manoeuvres and many a husband's career has been furthered through socialization channels, an aspect which is of unequalled importance in Philippine business. In the Philippines, how well you perform at work is of less importance than how well you get along with others. So to get anywhere in the business world (or in any other area for that matter), it is imperative that you be a good socializer. That is where the Filipino wife and/or mother can be very useful and effective.

## FILIPINO MEN

Regarding the Filipino male, Dr Lapuz states that 'the ego-ideal for men is that of one who is cool, cautious, inoffensive, pleasant, relaxed to the point of being rather easygoing, incapable of anger except when his *amor-propio* ... is provoked. His masculinity is definitely and emphatically regarded as intrinsic to this narcissism (self-esteem). Of this masculinity he is quite conscious and proud, and will emphasize it in many subtle and not-so-subtle ways. Outside of this ego-ideal, the Filipino male may appear to some, and in particular to foreigners, as not being masculine enough. He tends to be fastidious about his appearance, particularly his hair and clothes, to have soft and graceful movements. With strangers and in some unfamiliar situations, he may tend to say very little and act even less, which is the antithesis of the American male's tendency to quickly state his identity and give his opinion. The Filipino will be quiet and will strive to be inoffensive in situations where an American would feel obliged to be more vociferous.'

This description presents the outward or surface differences between Filipinos and Westerners, those noticed first. Psychological and personality differences, which are less noticeable in the first few interactions, are harder to recognize and grasp. To get a deeper insight into the Filipino male personality, it is necessary to look at the different roles he plays, because much of his behaviour and attitudes is determined by the duties which accompany each role. Some of the more important roles he plays are described here.

197

## *The Son*

The role of the Filipino son or, more specifically, the role of a 'good' Filipino son is placed above all the other male roles. It is more important to be a good son than a good father or a good husband. Filipinos stress the importance of remembering your past, where you came from and what your parents have done for you.

The farmer's lad who becomes a rich and famous doctor will buy his parents a nice house in the city or, if they don't want to move, will visit them once a week and give material support, possibly expanding the farm into a great *hacienda*. If his parents put him through medical school, he owes them even more. Being a doctor, he would have to personally see to his parents whenever they need any medical aid. (He also becomes the personal physician of the rest of the family—by the Filipino definition of the word, a service for which he never charges and which is often a personal inconvenience.) His great accomplishments as a doctor are nothing if he does not perform his duties as a son. First he must be a good son. Then, and only then, may he be successful.

Unlike American and other Western cultures, where sons are pushed to early autonomy, independence is not a matter of urgency. In some cases it is not an issue at all. Sons are not expected to leave the family home, fend for themselves and find their own place in life. They are expected to help their parents on the farm or in the family business when they are old enough while continuing to live off, and with, their parents.

It is when the son himself attempts autonomy and independence that commotion arises. Such a move is interpreted by the parents to mean he does not like living with them. The parents take a what's-wrong-with-us-don't-you-love-us-anymore attitude. They also worry that the neighbours will think they cannot support their children, marking them as parent failures. Most Filipino sons live with their parents until they get married. Where a son leaves school early to get a job, it would be because the father is unable to support the family due to illness or death, or his pay is inadequate to cover the costs involved in bringing up a large family. It is usually the eldest son who is assigned this duty.

Note the cultural difference here: the American boy leaves home to get a job to support himself thus lightening his father's burden; the Filipino boy leaves home to get a job in the city so he can support not only his parents but all his brothers and sisters. You will find many drivers, maids, salesgirls, etc. in Manila who are working so they can put their younger brothers and sisters through school.

The difference in cultural emphasis—autonomy (American) vs dependence (Filipino)—is illustrated by Dr Lapuz's example: 'In American culture, parents force autonomy upon their offspring at an early age with early severance of dependency ties. It is not unusual, for example, to see young people with moneyed parents working in order to have money of their own. In the Philippines, if a boy has parents with money, it hardly occurs to him to work. Sons are expected to grow up loyal to their parents, look after them, help younger siblings and generally be unselfish.'

## The Adolescent Male

Young Filipinos have a long adolescence. They enjoy a long 'period of immunity'—a time when adolescents can get away with childish, irresponsible behaviour because they are not yet considered adults and therefore not expected to behave accordingly. Most Filipino boys remain dependent on their parents until they marry or at least finish their schooling, which for the majority is at the completion of four or five years of tertiary education.

As most Filipino boys do not have to work their way through college, they have a lot of time to spend with friends. Peers figure largely in this phase. There is usually a prominent peer group called a *barkada* to which one belongs. These cliques or *barkadas* are tightly knit—the members are very close to each other and go everywhere together. They develop their own slang, they have

199

private jokes. They exercise control over the behaviour of members, mainly by teasing. There is usually no formal leader, though there may be one or two more respected members.

The *barkada* can be a powerful force. It operates on the principles of group pressure and conformity. For example, the group may resent a member having a girlfriend because he is not spending as much time with them, forcing him to choose between his girlfriend and his *barkada*. Or a member may be pressured into drinking, smoking or doing something he would normally not approve of. Because of the Filipino's need to belong to someone, the *barkada* is an essential part of an adolescent's life. Not to belong to any group is to feel like an outcast—loners and individualists (those who want to be different) are considered 'weird' by Filipinos. The society exerts tremendous pressure to conform. Once one belongs to a *barkada* one is ensured support and the fun of shared experiences.

Filipinos do not like being alone, perhaps because of the population density and the fact that from birth they are constantly surrounded by people. They do not like eating alone, they will not see a movie alone, they always have to be with someone—a friend or a relative. They do not enjoy experiences not shared with others. They feel uncomfortable eating beside someone who is not, so they will always offer to share their food or cajole their companion into having 'a bit of something'. The Filipino will not try anything new alone but with his *barkada* to back him up, he will.

Girls also have *barkadas* which perform the same functions as those described above, the only differences being due to differences in sex roles. Often, *barkadas* of opposite sexes will go out together and this is the usual social avenue for young people to meet.

## The Husband

The role of the Filipino husband is mainly that of breadwinner. This is the only duty he is really expected to fulfill and his performance in this area is what determines his success or failure as a husband

(and a father). A husband who has a mistress or *querida* is accepted and tolerated by society if he can support both his wife and mistress. A man who can support two or more families is regarded with amazement and admiration, not disgust, and earns a reputation for being macho. However, the playboy who goes around getting girls into trouble and then leaving them to fend for themselves is considered irresponsible and a coward.

In *A Study of Psychopathology*, Dr Lapuz says: 'The usual cultural norm for masculinity is firstly, the ability to perform sexual intercourse and secondly, freedom from marital controls in a man's activities.' The first criterion is measured by the number of children a man has, which is why large families are preferred in the Philippines. A large number of offspring is evidence of a man's virility. It also explains why a man will have children by his mistress.

The second norm is one that every Filipino husband strives to give an impression of, for fear of being called 'under the *saya*'— henpecked. This threat is real because Filipino wives are very dominant and, though they may appear quiet and submissive before others, are very skilful in manipulating their husbands to get what they want. Because the wife runs the household, she considers it her territory and the husband does not have much say in household issues. He gives his opinion only when consulted and even then his recommendations may not be followed. Thus, the Filipino husband concentrates on being a good provider for his wife and children.

## The Father

The breadwinner role played by the husband is extended to his role as a father. The father's main duty is to provide for his family as well as he can. It is a proud father who can say he put all his children through school and an even prouder one who can boast of seeing his children through college. Education is considered the best gift parents can give their children.

Many Filipino fathers also see it as their role to build up a business to ensure their children a place in life when they grow up and join the workforce. It is seen as an inheritance they can leave to their children upon their death. It is important to Filipinos that they leave something to their children—through this they feel they are continuing to provide for their children even when the latter are able to provide for themselves. Parents think it is their duty to give their children a better life than the one they had. This is how the present dynasties in the Philippines were built—a family business passed from generation to generation with each generation improving and expanding it. In leaving his children more than he received, a Filipino feels he has been a good father.

The Filipino father is a ceremonial figurehead. He is the head of the family, but in many cases, in name only. He is treated like royalty at home—the children must be quiet when he is asleep, they bring him his slippers when he gets home, cater to his whims and needs and take pains not to get in his way or arouse his anger because he works hard all day and needs to rest and relax. Hence they do not usually consult him about their problems. As a father he does not usually have much to do with the children's upbringing. That responsibility is designated to the mother.

The father is a disciplinary figure used by the mother to threaten the child into obedience, e.g. she might say 'stop teasing your sister or your father will belt you when he comes home'. This sometimes results in the children growing up in fear of their father and never getting to know him as a person. The Filipino only plays the role of father when his children are in their teenage years, whereupon he becomes more aware and more controlling of their activities. His role as disciplinarian is even stronger now because the wife seems to feel less capable in this area once the children are older. This is due to the disciplinary methods she uses (threats and bribery) which become less effective when the children get older. But the Filipino father's most important role or duty is still that of provider and the role is a lifetime one.

## Lolo: *The Grandfather*

Elders are respected and revered. The grandfather heads the hierarchy in the family structure and may be likened to an old tribal chief. His advice and opinions on a wide variety of matters are sought by the younger family members. He takes great interest in his grandchildren and may sponsor a favourite grandchild through college in Manila or even abroad. The role of ceremonial figurehead is maintained, but this time over a larger fiefdom.

*Elders are respected by Filipinos as the repositories of tradition, the living links to family roots. Ifugao elders, such as this man, proffer advice and serve as middlemen to settle disputes.*

## Bakla: *The Homosexual*

Homosexuals are accepted and tolerated by Philippine society. In fact, they have their own functions and roles to perform. The term 'homosexual' as used here does not distinguish between different types of homosexuals. Most prominent are the male homosexuals but gay females are also accepted and tolerated. The *bakla* or male homosexual who acts like a female is a figure of fun in movies and television shows. But the important role they assume in society is that of arbiter of taste. They are the couturiers, interior decorators, architects, hairdressers and make-up artists. Women look to them for setting the trend in fashion and design, often trusting their judgment more than their own.

They are thus very much a part of Philippine society and one will encounter them everywhere. They have their own language, swardspeak, their own way of speaking and their own mannerisms, different to those of females. They are fun-loving, entertaining and are many a girl's best friend as they sometimes play the role of confidante to women. Even the men banter with them, teasing and making fun of them, though with no malicious intent.

# Chapter Ten

# GUIDE TO PECULIARLY FILIPINO WAYS

Running amok.

## *Amok and* Juramentado

Said to be a Malay phenomenon, psychologists claim Filipinos go amok because the society represses expressions of hostility. The banking of resentment (*nagtatanim ng galit*, meaning seeding anger) builds up to an explosive point and the amok unleashes pent-up violence, usually with *bolo* or knife, on anyone near by, often his own kin. After the incident the amok is unaware of what he has done, differentiating him from the Western individual who goes berserk.

Among Muslim Filipinos, the amok went through a religious

ritual obtaining the approval of the Imam (priest). Bidding farewell to his family, he was given the full ritual for the dead, his eyebrows shaved, his body washed and clothed in white. The Muslim amok was a phenomenon during the period of armed struggle against the Spanish and American colonizers. Aside from psychological reasons the amok had religious motivation, attacking 'evil' enemies of his Islamic faith in order to die an innocent 'good death'. The word *juramentado* is Spanish for one who has taken a solemn oath to do violence until death; Muslims call the action *parrang sabbil*, meaning a war in the path of Allah.

## Bahala Na: *Fatalism or Resignation?*

This trait, said to imply fatalism, literally means leaving things to *Bahala* (god) or 'let the circumstance take care of itself'. As Filipinos rely on the goodwill of other people, such as their superiors, to do what is right by them, and as within a tight kinship the individual has to accommodate and defer to so many other interests and opinions, *bahala na* may also be another way of avoiding hopelessly long and entangled decision-making. *Bahala na* is the Filipino 'too hard' basket, where planning and worrying are shelved because it depends not on him but on other persons, minds, and whims.

## Bakla

Homosexuals are viewed with much tolerance. People make fun of them, but do not harshly censure homosexual behaviour. Like the *querida* system, real homosexuality is below the surface, overt manifestations such as transvestism are humoured. Remember, however, that a male arm on another man's shoulders, and males holding hands, are not considered gay.

## Balato

Anyone who enjoys a windfall, from a bet or an unexpected financial reward, is cajoled into sharing a bit with kin and friends as *balato*.

## Balimbing

A reference to the many-sided star fruit, the term is applied to someone who changes allegiance for personal convenience. The allusion is that the person is not only double-faced, but multiple-faced. Despite clear lines evolving between Marcos cronies and enemies during martial law, the Aquino government has legitimized and even crowned the *balimbing*. Erap Estrada continues the tradition.

## Bangungot

Rare disease said to be peculiar to Filipino bachelors aged 25–40. They go to sleep and are found dead next morning, apparently after a violent nightmare. Filipinos blame it on heavy meals before bedtime or a demon who sits on the chest; researchers tried to trace it to such Filipino foods as *bagoong* and *patis*, but no culprit or virus has been isolated. It has also been reported among Filipinos in Hawaii (84 deaths in 1937–48 recorded by the city pathologist in Honolulu).

## Bayanihan

Traditional working-together method in rural areas for work requiring many hands, such as planting and harvesting. When a villager has to move his house (literally carrying it on its main posts), the community helps. The house-owner offers some refreshments and would offer similar help for those in the same predicament. The term symbolizes the Filipino capacity to work together for a civic end.

*Moving house in rural Philippines is literally picking up the house and transferring it to another site.*

## *Blow-out*

Another form of sharing a windfall (see *balato*) or celebrating some happy event is by giving friends a treat at a restaurant or a feast at home called a 'blow-out'.

## *Born Again*

A religious movement brought in from the USA; the Filipino adaptation includes both Catholic and Protestant groups, marking a resurgence of religious conservatism. It has many forms in the Philippines, and diverse religious fundamentalists immerse themselves in prayer meetings, bible studies and so on. The phenomenal growth of born-again persons and movements reveals the resurgence of religious fervour among Filipinos.

## *Debate:* **Balagtasan**

Philippine traditional debate concerns itself with form, not substance; with delivery and flowery imagery, not with logic and issues. It is not so much *what* you say as *how* you say it. Poetical jousts enjoyed great popularity in the past and still do in small old towns. Because smooth interpersonal relations prohibit sharp, cutting debate, the clash of ideas never seems to appeal too strongly to Filipinos, who enjoy more the right phrase to win friends, the apt imagery to produce smiles, the perfect foil to turn away anger.

Serious debate and confrontation of ideas in conferences and forums are not likely to flourish. The chairman in a seminar is more concerned about deflecting and burying direct confrontation than bringing matters to a head. Debaters are so effusive about sugar-coating and watering down their own arguments to avoid offence and ruffled feelings that nothing is really said in the end.

## Despedida

One who is leaving for a long period is given a special feast called a *despedida* (Spanish for farewell). Close friends are invited and the departing guest of honour may submit names of friends to be invited.

## *Face:* Mukha

Filipinos emphasize appearances. They make a clear distinction between public front and inner self. Husbands never confide in anyone about wives' failings because that would reveal their own weakness. You could have a lifelong association with a colleague who has several mistresses and never mention the subject. Unhappy marriages have a lifelong public existence despite private misery because of appearances.

For some Filipinos, appearances become all that matter, foisting illusions as the substance of real accomplishments. Filipinos refer to such superficiality as *balatkayo* (hypocrite), *pabalatbunga* (fruit skin), *pakitang-tao* (public show). Consequently, they value a person for his inner self (*loob*) and assess his character by his *loob*.

## *Faithhealer*

Filipino faithhealers are reputed to possess psychic healing powers. They are said to operate without instruments, close wounds and leave no scars, and cure through divine aid. When a healer loses his powers, it is allegedly due to exhaustion of energy or his having become mercenary. One famous faithhealer did not hesitate to go to hospital for an appendicectomy which may, or may not, say something about faithhealing. The tradition goes back several centuries.

## *Fast Sprinters:* Ningas Kugon

Many projects start like a house on fire only to sputter out midway. The tendency to lose enthusiasm halfway through a project has been likened to grassfire (*ningas kugon*) burning itself out quickly. Stamina is lost upon meeting an obstacle. One reason is that smooth interpersonal relations do not really thresh out objections, criticisms and misgivings about a project. Filipinos tend to agree and see only the bright side of proposals, yielding their misgivings to the leader's enthusiasm. When difficulties arise, commitment to the project is tested, and most are found to have given only token assent.

Filipinos rely very strongly on the personality of the leader, and obviously a programme gains ready support among the leader's kin group and friends, but once the programme goes out into the community itself it may not get the same response. Unless others pick up the ball, it comes to a halt.

## First Lady

A quasi-official office, the role of the wife of the President of the Philippines exudes an aura of charm and power. Filipinos see the wife of a head of state, and wives of ministers and other public officials as well, as enjoying the same power and influence over her husband as other Filipinas in their homes. A First Lady is expected to be endowed with grace and charm (if she is beautiful and can sing, glorious), help her husband win votes, and influence her husband's official policies. The perfect Filipino go-between. She functions in her own sphere of activity, such as in civic projects.

## Food

The importance of food in the Filipino psyche cannot be underestimated. He fears running short of food, and everywhere he goes the Filipino must have, as a security blanket, abundant provisions to reassure him that he will not starve to death. A sojourn to the beach which consists of a safari of food bundles, will not seem sufficient unless there are stops at fruit stores for more supplies. Even a trip to see a movie will require provisions.

There is no gathering of Filipinos without food. It is standard hospitality to offer visitors not just a drink but food, be it only biscuits or rice cakes. The usual Filipino greeting is 'Have you eaten?' (*Kumain ka na ba*?) Eating in front of others and not offering a share is rude. A driver not given his meal on time has his driving impaired. The most constant and visible growth in Metro Manila has been in eateries. And try getting service from a clerk eating lunch at her desk, or a bureaucrat at his coffee break!

## *The Great Sulk:* Tampo

Since Filipinos are not allowed to express anger or resentment, sublimated hostility takes the form of sulking and withdrawal of customary cheerfulness in the presence of one who has displeased them. These are signals for the offender to restore goodwill, not necessarily by talking out the problem, but by showing concern about the wounded person's well-being. If the silent treatment goes unnoticed, then a few grumbling sounds, a door slammed, a foot stomped, and barely audible mutterings under the breath—a more open form of sulking or *nagdadabog*—follow. It is important to respond to these with friendly overtures or relations will deteriorate. Filipinos allow a bit of time for 'cooling off' before responding.

## Kurakot

To rake in payola and amass megawealth through graft and corruption. While graft and corruption were rampant before the Marcos regime, immunity from public exposure and accountability during martial law (1972–86) pushed the greed lever to maximum, making the amassing of ill-gotten wealth a nearly institutionalized industry among the favoured few who were called cronies. The legacy of the Marcos years remains very much in the country.

## *Micro-retail:* Tingi

Philippine commerce deals with the smallest unit possible, one cigarette stick, one piece of chewing gum, one garlic clove, one small cup of vinegar, one pat of lard. Jeepney drivers who buy one cigarette have their purchase lighted for them. Where contemporary retail markets emphasize bulk quantity purchase, the Filipino consumer seems inclined to purchase the minimum quantity.

## *Motel*

Not a hotel for weary automobile travellers. Its unique architecture is designed for discreet trysts. High walls permit entrance and exit with minimum visibility. The individual single car garage has stairs leading directly to a room. Motels are essentially for love trysts and the charge is by the hour. Female passengers leaving motels are extremely literate, wear dark glasses and always read large newspapers close to their face on the way out.

## *One, Two, Three*

Filipino con-games, popularly called 'one, two, three', thrive in the cities. A common one is a device that can duplicate peso bills. Burglars gain entry into homes when owners are away by telling the househelp they are there to pick up the television set or some other appliance for repairs. Another *modus operandi* is to call up the househelp or kin while the owner is away to report that the owner has just had a serious car accident and urgently needs money (for blood or emergency treatment), which they must frantically search for in safeboxes or locked drawers in the house and give to the caller who will meet them at a designated place immediately.

## Pabaon

An old Filipino custom gives departing guests a small parcel of food from the feast. It is the proper send-off gesture, even for kin leaving the country. Archaeologists refer to food offerings on pottery and porcelain ware in ancient gravesites as *pabaon*.

## Palakasan

The dynamics of power often functions through political influence. *Malakas* (strong) implies one who is powerful and uses his powers to gain his ends. *Malakas* also means someone close to, or influential with, a power figure or an institution. The ruthless and wanton use of political office or power is epitomized by one politician's unhappy, much quoted, comment: 'What are we in power for?' To be law-abiding or unwilling to cow people with power is *mahina* (weak). *Palakasan* is a system of survival of the most politically influential.

## Pasalubong *Travellers*

Travellers or holiday-makers bring back gifts for kin and friends, even if the trip is just to a nearby town: some special food the place is noted for—strawberries from Baguio, pineapple from Tagaytay, Ojaldres biscuits from the Visayas, pastillas from Bulacan, turron from Pampanga ... Travelling abroad is often a shopping chore for a list of relatives' and friends' *pasalubong*—a greeting gift.

## *People Power*

The historic event which led to the fall of Marcos and the restoration of democracy is attributed to non-violent public demonstrations that pressured Marcos to hold a snap election resulting in the events which pitted unarmed civilians against armoured carriers and marines in full battle gear along the thoroughfare known as EDSA.

## *Point of No Return:* Napasubo

*Hiya* and *amor-propio* create situations where one is publicly committed to a stand and cannot back out of it. The Filipino will stonewall it through, because he is *napasubo*—committed.

## *Propriety:* Delicadeza

A Spanish loan value, popular among the genteel class of Filipinos as a built-in self-imposed sense of proper decorum, like the European noblesse oblige, controlling behaviour. It is no longer in vogue.

## *The* Querida *System*

A lax marital standard exists for the Filipino male, who often acquires a mistress with whom he starts a second family. There are those who see macho qualities in this lifestyle. From powerful and wealthy young technocrats to the lowliest traffic cop and jeepney driver, the practice is widespread. Legitimate wives live with the hazard of sharing their virile husbands with sub rosa rivals. Philippine law recognizes the rights of a mistress who has cohabited with a man for seven years, and illegitimate children who carry the father's name have claims to inheritance. Thus even after the death of the macho husband, rivalry over the funeral services, and of course the worldly possessions he left behind, follow.

The *querida* system is not discussed in public as it carries formal social censure. It is tolerated and whispered about in private. A friend or kin may bring up his 'number two' in conversation with you, but you may not. For public consumption it does not exist.

Filipinos tend to see marital straying by the husband as a failure of the wife; she is either too nice to him or not nice enough, has neglected to keep herself sexually attractive or devotes too much time to looking attractive instead of attending to the house. For some, having a number two, or three, or more, is a status symbol equated with success. It must also be said that these macho types are usually attentive to family obligations, to both wife and 'numbers'.

Wives may complain and women's lib foam at the mouth; the fact is that the *querida* system is kept alive by all those women who are happy to be numbers two and three, who number more than the macho husbands. The Westerner should however not be misled into thinking this is a socially accepted practice, or that women he meets are dying to become mistresses. It is an underground life. A mistress has no social acceptance, no matter how powerful her lover and how brazenly she flaunts her status; people may be civil, but she enjoys no public esteem. When you consider how important *amor-propio*, *hiya*, and public acceptance is to the Filipino, the mistress does not exist as a person in the society. She has been given various appellations: *querida* (Spanish for 'loved one') has been corrupted to *kiri*; she is also *kulasisi*, a small green parrot people keep for amusement, and *kalapating mababang lipad*, a low-flying dove.

'A busy left hand which the right hand is unaware of' is the metaphor for marital infidelity (*nangangaliwa*) and while 'left-handed' husbands are tolerated, society is short-tempered with regard to wifely 'left turns'.

## The Queue

Filipinos do not like to queue. In World War II the Japanese tried to get them to queue up for direly needed rice rations, and they regard queuing as the pits of wartime days. The water shortage in postwar Manila created queues for water in congested areas, again the depths of despair. The *pila* (queue) is something you try to avoid.

An American explained a technique Filipinos use to get through a crowd when no queue is visible. He thrusts himself, elbow first, through an opening, making sure he is not looking at the person he is nudging, and then swings his body and thrusts the other elbow through, this time looking in the other direction, and so on down through the crowd. Those nudged will look at the source of intrusion but will not be offended because the nudger is not facing them.

## Salvage

Death squad term for assassination, used by the military during Marcos's martial law years to exterminate troublesome activists and oppositionists, mostly peasant and labour leaders.

## Scoring Freebies: Lista Sa Tubig

Kinship sharing is a rule. One measure of closeness to someone is willingness to share. To have to pay for a book, a painting, or a candy bar from an author, painter, or shopowner friend, would mean one is like other mortals, not a special kin or friend. Filipinos are inclined to help themselves with the expectation they will not be charged or you will not object if you are a close relative or friend. Some expressions used for this are: 'T.Y.' (thank you), 'ambush', '*lista sa tubig*' (write the credit account on water) and '*dilihensiya*'.

## Suki

Filipinos like to build personal bonds even in business; and in the small retail trade, buyers favour shopowners who show them preference, offering the best quality at special prices and permitting purchase on credit in return for loyal patronage. The relationship, *suki*, is common between housewives and market vendors.

## Superstitions and Mythology

**KULAM** Unexplained maladies are commonly attributed to *kulam*, a form of sorcery. It is believed psychic people can cause illness by a stare. The *mangkukulam* apparently does his evil deed because of some trivial offence, real or imagined, or purely out of whim.

**ASWANG** A creature of the netherworld, the *aswang* is evil, at times taking the form of a pig, a dog, or a nocturnal bird called *tik-tik*. While capable of doing harm to anyone, the *aswang's* favourite prey is the pregnant woman because he eats live human foetuses.

**MANANANGGAL** Female vampire who can disengage the top half of her body and fly at night to the beds of unsuspecting sleeping men, her usual victims. Place salt on the severed half-torso to slay her should you learn your wife is really a *manananggal*.

**NUNO SA PUNSO** A tiny old man who squats on an anthill and has magic powers that could cause you good or ill fortune. You should always ask his permission when passing an anthill.

**ANTING-ANTING** Belief in *anting-anting* (amulets or talismans) was noted by Spanish chroniclers. Today it is widespread. *Anting-anting* of Christian Filipinos may have Christian symbols and Latin names in corrupt form. It can make one invincible, or invisible. *Anting-anting* also refers to lucky charms for prosperity or fertility. It is the warrior's secret weapon; notorious bandits were believed to own specially potent *anting-anting*. Religious folk cults carry *anting-anting*. The former President's biographer, Hartzell Spence, claims Marcos had one inserted in his back by Bishop Aglipay.

**GAYUMA** Love charms may help win the affections of one's object of desire. One who acts lovesick or is attracted to an unexpected 'mismatch' is said to have been under a love spell (*nagayuma*).

**TO STOP RAIN** If you are giving a garden party and it looks like rain, send some eggs to Santa Clara. The Sisters of Saint Claire are happy to receive the eggs, but make no guarantee of sunshine.

NUMEROLOGY Some Filipinos are wary of number 13, and will avoid entertaining 13 at a table. Steps to the main entrance of a house should not fall on a number divisible by three. Count *oro, plata, mata* as you descend; the last step should not end with *mata*.

LENTEN TABOOS Lent is full of omens. Superstitious folk will not travel or bathe on Holy Thursday and Good Friday. People test their *anting-anting* on Good Friday. On Holy Saturday, at Mass, if children jump up high during the offertory, they will grow tall.

## *Tao*

*Tao*, meaning person, is used in various forms, all stressing human dignity or frailty. Human weakness is justified by 'We are only *tao*'. *Tao* is also used to refer to the common man, the peasant, the worker. Someone announcing his presence in someone else's house will knock and say '*Tao po*', meaning 'A person is here, sir.'

## *Trapo*

Acronym for TRAditional POlitician in direct reference to public officials who returned after the Marcos dictatorship to restore the discredited political system that Marcos used to justify military rule. Indeed, while there is, unhappily, an abundance of *trapos*, no real alternative type of public official has emerged who can be classified as different from any other *trapo*, which, incidentally, is Tagalog for 'rags'.

## *Under the* Saya

The Filipino macho cult is checkmated by strong-willed wives who keep their husbands humble, and these henpecked husbands are teased as living under their wives' skirts (under the *saya*).

## *Vigilante*

Anti-communist group or movement with quasi-official links who employ death-squad tactics against alleged communists.

# CULTURAL QUIZ

Test your ability to adapt to Philippine situations, bearing in mind that black and white answers are not as important as being able to play by Philippine society's rules.

## SITUATION 1

An armed soldier, a little drunk, takes a seat in front of you in a jeepney, and he catches your eye. Do you:

*A* Stare back at him expressing your disapproval.
*B* Look away and pretend he is not there.
*C* Smile and start a conversation with him.

## Comments

Look away. Staring (*A*) would be provocative and invite a quarrel. Smiling (*C*) may be friendly but could be interpreted as mocking him and, in any case, opening a conversation with an armed drunk is always unpredictable.

## SITUATION 2

You enter your employee's home and he is having dinner, and he says, 'Have something to eat.' Do you say:

A  Yes, thank you, I'm starving.
B  No, thank you, I have just had dinner.
C  I'll just have a drink, thanks.

## Comments

Accepting outright would catch him off-guard. The invitation was purely formal courtesy, not to be taken literally, so acceptance could place him in an embarrassing situation, especially if he thinks what he has may not be good enough for you (Filipinos always prepare special food for guests). Only if he insists and repeats the offer would it be proper to accept. (Inversely, most Filipinos decline a first offer of coffee, or a cigarette, expecting the offer to be repeated before saying *yes*.) 'No, thanks' is therefore the expected answer. Option (C), however, is also acceptable in most situations.

## SITUATION 3

Your househelp comes to you with a story about a sick relative and asks for a substantial loan; she has previously borrowed, and still owes you, the equivalent of three months' wages. Do you:

A  Lend the money to help the poor woman.
B  Lend only a partial amount.
C  Refuse to loan her any more because you have rules about loans of more than the equivalent of three months' wages.

## Comments

Your chances of recovering a loan of six months' wages are very slim indeed. Furthermore, the househelp, heavily in debt, will lose incentive to work as most of her wages will only go towards paying the loan. Giving a partial loan will not really solve her problem, as kinfolk in economic need is a perennial condition. If you have great confidence in the househelp, and value her service, you might take the partial loan risk. It is best to invoke your own rules and say you cannot lend any more as this is readily understood by househelp.

## SITUATION 4

You have been invited to the house of a prominent official for dinner. When taking your leave, do you:

A Compliment the host's wife for cooking an excellent dinner.

B Compliment her on her choice of chef.

C Compliment her on her lovely home and the fine dinner in general.

## Comments

Wealthy wives hire cooks to prepare meals, so a compliment to the host's wife is probably misdirected unless she has informed you personally that she cooked the meal or one course. B would be taken as a left-handed compliment and not earn you any points. Commenting on the lovely appearance of her home and the general supervision and presentation of the dinner gives her the proper credit, and would be appreciated.

## SITUATION 5

All your friends talk about a Filipino friend's affair with a mistress; the next time you see him do you:

A  Ask him how his mistress is.
B  Inform him of all the gossip you have heard about him.
C  Avoid any mention of his private love life.

### Comments

Husbands who stray are regarded as 'macho' by friends, but their peccadilloes are considered not socially acceptable. Therefore, you can discuss such delicate matters with a friend only if he brings up the subject himself. He would consider you forward and a busybody to ask how she is (A), and he would be uncomfortable learning of gossip about him, but will not think you are doing him a favour. He may think your open knowledge of his affair may lower your respect for him, affecting your friendship. It's a subject you had better avoid mentioning.

## *HOUSE-HUNTING*

You are looking for a house or an apartment to live in. Which of the following would you consider when making your choice?

1 A view of Manila Bay.
2 Downtown location.
3 Security.
4 Carpets and good facilities.
5 A modern kitchen and laundry machine.
6 Propensity for flooding in house, yard, and street during heavy rains.
7 Telephone facilities.
8 Traffic-free accessibility to place of work and children's school.
9 Open gardens, open windows for ventilation.
10 Secluded, very private location.

Perfect!

## *Comments*

The good view is a bonus but has to take low priority. A downtown location is fine, but beware of being trapped in traffic-clogged downtown areas. Security is very important as burglaries are rampant. Carpets and modern fixtures are good only if they are in airconditioned quarters; with the frequent power failures and escalating cost of electricity, they may prove inessential. A modern kitchen and laundry machine are only useful if you will personally use them, but hired help is so readily available and inexpensive—the one great asset of living in the Philippines—that these technical gadgets should have low priority. Flooding is a different matter. Check carefully the premises you are moving into, as if you were buying seashore land that could vanish with a high tide.

Telephone facilities are a must. Getting a new line installed could take a very long time. A party-line telephone is not recommended. If you can afford two telephones, get them. It is important to consider movement in the streets because rush hour traffic could consume all your time getting to work and back. If you have children who go to school this should be considered also. Open gardens and open windows look very nice and comfortable, but conflict with the need to provide for security, including high walls, gates, window bars, and door locks. For this same reason a secluded, private place may invite intrusion by burglars and other unwanted criminals.

The answers, in descending order of importance: 3, 6, 7, 8, 1, 2, 4, 5, 9, 10.

## THE ANSWER 'YES'

Which of the following would the Filipino 'yes' mean?
1 I don't know.
2 Maybe.
3 If you say so.
4 Go soak your head.
5 Yes, of course.
6 Let me out of here.
7 Where's the men's room?
8 No, but I won't openly disagree with you.
9 Do you realize what time it is?
10 You foreigners are all alike.

## Comments

A 'yes' can mean many things depending on the expression that goes with it and the voice intonation. It is not a fixed definition or manner, you have to send out your antennae and check out the circumstances. 'Yes' can be blurted out because the househelp is confused and will not say so. 'Yes' can also mean he does not understand what you just said but is embarrassed to admit it. 'Yes' can be said just to please you at the moment. However, the answers 4, 6, 7, 9 and 10 are beyond the limits of a Filipino 'yes'.

## *TRUE OR FALSE?*

Here is a simple true-or-false test to get you warmed up and to gauge your understanding of life in the Philippines.

1 When commemorating the anniversary of the dead on 'All Souls Day', it is definitely not proper to bring food and eat near the tombstones.

2 Prices in general retail business, such as in public markets, are fixed and one should never haggle.

3 Men and women never publicly touch each other, but people of the same sex often do.

4 People judge you by your appearance.

5 Christians are a minority in the Philippines.

6 Filipino peasants eat with their fingers.

7 Manila's University of Santo Thomas is older than America's Harvard University.

8 A boy and a girl should not kiss on their first date.

9 Office workers consider afternoon tea or *merienda* an institution conducive to good working conditions.

10 It is safe to leave expensive items in your yard or unlocked car.

### *Answers*

False: 1, 2, 5, 10
True: 3, 4, 6, 7, 8, 9

## *PRIORITIES*

When working with Filipinos it is important to consider their own concept of priorities, that which they deem important as against what a foreigner values. In the following list of values and virtues, check the ten traits that Filipinos would consider most important.

1 Verbal, face-to-face candour.
2 Rugged individualism.
3 Family ties.
4 Being a good son.
5 Beauty and elegance.
6 Consensus and group agreement.
7 Public image and what people say.
8 Gratitude for past favours, acknowledging this as a debt of honour.
9 Swift, objective action regardless of who gets hurt.
10 Personalized viewpoint.
11 Friendliness and conviviality.
12 Diplomacy.
13 Honour.
14 Efficiency.
15 Gentle manners.

### *Comments*

Most appealing:
3, 4, 5, 6, 7, 8,
11, 12, 13, 15
Least appealing:
1, 2, 9, 10, 14

227

## *DESIRABILITY FACTOR*

Out of the following list of ten, check the five negative traits Filipinos consider highly objectionable and undesirable.

1 Ingratitude.
2 Lack of punctuality.
3 Evasiveness.
4 Public belligerence.
5 Lack of shame.
6 Inability to get along with others.
7 Nepotism.
8 Going by the book.
9 Dishonesty.
10 Philandering.

### *Comments*

Most desirable: 1, 4, 5, 6, 8
Dishonesty would be frowned on, but the other negative traits would be shrugged off as part of human weakness.

## *A HOUSEHOLD MAZE*

Try going through a series of typical Filipino situations.

Your househelp sees a dress of yours lying discarded on the floor in your room; thinking it is meant to be laundered, she puts it in with the rest of the laundry. Unfortunately, it is supposed to be dry-cleaned only, and it comes back ruined. It was an expensive dress, one of your favourites. You had taken particular care not to put it in with the rest of your laundry precisely to avoid such a catastrophe. How do you deal with the maid's error? Do you:

1 Reprimand her loudly and in public, telling her she should never take the liberty of washing clothes she finds lying in the room, and that the least she should have done was to read the washing instructions on the label? If so, proceed to *A*.

2 Talk to her privately, explain what she has done wrong, and advise her that the next time she should ask you first before washing clothes she finds lying in the room; then show her how to read the washing instructions on the label to make sure it doesn't say 'dry-clean only'? If this is your choice, proceed to *B*.

3 Reprimand her in private and as a penalty deduct from her wages the cost of the dress? Go to *C*.

## A

Since reprimanding your househelp in public has caused her to lose face, to save face she threatens to quit. Do you:

1 Tell her in front of the household to leave immediately because she is incompetent? This answer takes you to *D*.

2 Persuade her to stay by talking to her privately, asking her what the problem is, and perhaps explaining that you were upset at the time, telling her to do the task correctly next time? Proceed to *E*.

3 Use a go-between, another househelp perhaps, to talk to her and persuade her to stay? This takes you to *E*.

Watch the label.

## B

Congratulations! Your patience will be rewarded. This is the right approach and it is most effective. Reprimanding her in private will allow her to keep her self-respect with her fellow househelp. By explaining quietly what she has done wrong and showing her how to do it properly, you will prevent another accident of this nature. Checking labels for washing instructions will be a practice she probably does not know about. Welcome to Philippine living.

## C

Reprimanding her in private is the right approach. However, as you are making her pay for it, she now loses interest in her job because she is no longer getting much remuneration, if any, out of it. The proportion between her small salary and the cost of the expensive clothes you wear will seem to her truly unjust. Now you find you are getting very poor service from her, and even that is given grudgingly. You therefore decide to fire her. How do you go about this? Do you:

1 Take her aside, give her one month's pay, and say quietly, 'Obviously you are not happy here, so I will let you off'? This reply takes you to *F*.

2  Make a big scene, yell and fire her in public, pointing out all the errors she has made in the last two weeks? This answer takes you to *D*.

## D

This approach is not recommended. Expect the following repercussions:

1  The cook, who is her cousin or townmate, will also leave in sympathy.
2  Out of spite, she may damage your property before she leaves. (After all, what has she got to lose?)
3  She will spread unsavoury stories about you to the other househelp in the neighbourhood.

Therefore, go back to *C* where you erred, and try another approach.

## E

Good! You are correcting the error you made in reprimanding her publicly. The use of a go-between is also an effective method of resolving the conflict. The go-between will probably persuade her to stay; in any case, the go-between will clarify and inform you of the maid's real grievances and feelings. You are operating in the Filipino way.

## F

This is the right approach. If you handle it sensitively, you will part amicably, with no ill feelings and no risk of some gesture of 'getting back at you' for the offence you have given her. Remember, once a conflict is open and public, it is difficult to resolve and can involve others in the kin group. Avoid bitterly emotional endings.

# DO'S AND DON'TS APPENDIX

## TRAVELLING
### Do

- Check on health hazards and the prevalence of malaria. As a precaution take flu shots as well as typhoid shots.
- Have handy some mild insect repellent
- Beware of pickpockets in crowds inside a church or in fancy shopping malls. You may find money belts more helpful than the police.
- Beware of crooks disguised as police in Metro Manila and other major cities. These crooks pretend to be looking for counterfeit bills and pressure their victim to let them go over their cash, or they 'check' a victim's passport and papers and refuse to hand these back unless a sum of money is handed over.
- Beware of touts who get friendly with you.

### Don't

- Eat fresh green salads in one-star eateries, and don't drink tap water. Note that bottled soft drinks when served in a glass will contain ice which could contain unboiled tap water.
- Travel at all to remote areas, say in Sulu and Basilan without first checking with the authorities and your embassy regarding the security conditions.
- Risk travel by inter-island ferry. Opt for a plane.
- Take return flights during inter-island travel for granted. Always reconfirm your return flight at the local airport.

- Leave your belongings unattended especially in crowded places.
- Humour drunks, beggars or louts in public places.

## LIVING IN THE PHILIPPINES
### Do

- Be alert to security aspects such as the type of neighbourhood and its surroundings, and the types of protection doors and windows have when you are finding a place to stay. Staying in a 'village' offers you protection, and is the common option for most expatriates.
- Consider the location of the house against the elements.
- Have back up in case of power failure, such as a generator, flash-lights and gas burners (for cooking).
- Remember time has a different framework in the Philippines. As a rule try to accomplish one important meeting or transaction a day, because that is all you probably will have time for.
- Stand when the national anthem is played before movie screenings.

### Don't

- Be offended if country folk stare at you and if you are Caucasian, call out "Hello Joe!" People still find strangers a curiosity.
- Stare back as this could be regarded as rude on your part (though not on theirs).
- Expect formal RSVP replies from Filipinos, but they will still show up.
- Expect punctuality. It is polite to be late.
- Expect a 'Dutch treat' system where each pays his/her own.

# GLOSSARY

***Abuloy*** Donation, used also in reference to contribution in a wake.

***Adobo*** Popular Filipino dish made of chicken and pork cooked in garlic, soy sauce and vinegar.

***Alkalde*** (Sp. *alcalde*) A mayor.

***Ambus*** From 'ambush', scoring a freebie.

***Amor-propio*** Self-respect.

***Anting-anting*** Amulet.

***Arte*** (Sp. artifice) Studied artificial mannerisms in reference to vain, self-conscious persons.

***Aswang*** Folkloric creature, preys on live human foetus in pregnant women.

***Ate*** Sister.

**Ati-atihan** Festival in Kalibo, Aklan commemorating, according to folk legend, a peace treaty between the Atis and the Malays.

***Atsay*** (Slang, vulgar, not polite) Maid.

***Babang luksa*** The time when mourning clothes are shed (traditionally on the first anniversary of the death).

***Baduy*** (Slang) In bad taste; pedestrian.

***Bagoong*** Shrimp paste.

***Bahala na*** (Idiom) 'Leave it to god' or 'let the circumstance take care of itself'.

***Bakla*** Homosexual (male).

***Bakya*** (Colloquial) Mass appeal; the word means wooden clogs, traditionally worn by the masses.

***Balagtasan*** Poetical debate.

***Balatkayo*** (1) False front; (adj.) hypocritical; (2) disguise.

***Balato*** Sharing a portion of a windfall.

*Balintawak* National dress for women; a close-fitting gown with butterfly sleeves.

*Balut* Boiled duck's egg with embryo.

*Bangungot* Rare disease peculiar to Filipino males where they go to sleep and are found dead the next morning, apparently after suffering a violent nightmare.

*Barangay* Traditionally a social unit making up the nucleus of villages and *barrios*; today, a political unit created by ex-President Marcos.

*Barkada* Close-knit group of friends.

*Barong-barong* Shanty.

*Barong tagalog* National dress for men; a loose-fitting embroidered shirt, with a slit on each side, worn over trousers.

*Barrio, Baryo* Suburban district of a municipality.

*Batalan* Rear platform of barrio house (nipa hut), for washing and storing water.

*Bayan* (1) Town, municipality; (2) country, nation.

*Bayanihan* (1) Working together for mutual benefit; community cooperation; (2) dance troupe made popular by the Philippine Women's University.

*Bienvenida* Homecoming party.

*Binata* Bachelor.

*Bisperas* The day before an affair; preparations before an event.

**Blowout** Treat in a restaurant or snack bar given by someone to celebrate personal good fortune.

**Blue lady** Member of the former First Lady's kitchen cabinet; the term originated from the blue dresses worn by prominent lady supporters of ex-President Marcos' candidacy.

**Boss** (Slang) Informal address used for policemen or people in a higher position than oneself, or in other circumstances, used to flatter.

**Brownout** Power failure in one city area.

*Carroza* Carriage upon which the figure of a saint is carried during religious processions.

*Casador* Bookkeeper at a cockfight; his job includes establishing the odds and covering all bets.

*Comadre, kumadre, kumare* Social bond established through sponsorship in baptism, wedding and confirmation ceremonies; females are called comadre.

*Compadre, kumpadre, kumpare* See comadre; male.

**CCP** Cultural Centre of the Philippines.

*Dalaga* Unmarried lady.

*Dato, datu* Tribal chief.

*Despedida* Farewell party.

*Despedida de soltera* Party given by the women of the bride's family to mark the end of her single life.

*Ewan* 'I don't know', an expression used to evade confrontation.

*Fiesta* Annual town festival, usually on the feast day of the town patron saint; a large celebration.

**Fix** (Colloquial) To settle legal difficulties outside of the system.

**Flores de Mayo** Festival in May.

**'For a while'** (Colloquial) 'Hold the line'; 'just a minute'; 'hang on'.

*Gayuma* Love charm or potion.

*Gigantes* Papier-mâché figures of giants worn during fiestas.

*Hacienda* Agricultural estate.

*Hermano mayor* Honorary position conferred on someone; the position involves hosting or sponsoring events or portions of the town fiesta.

*Hiya* Shame.

*Inaanak* Godchild.

*Inay, nanay* Mother.

*Itay, tatay* Father.

**Jeepney** Popular form of public transportation.

*Jota* (Sp.) Rural folkdance of Spanish influence using bamboo castanets.

*Juego de anillo* (Sp.) Game of Spanish influence played during fiestas wherein a person riding a horse (nowadays a bicycle) attempts to pierce a suspended ring with a stick.

*Kamayan* Eating with the hands (i.e., without cutlery).

*Kami* Pronoun 'we', used when the person addressed is not included. Compare this with *tayo*.

*Kano* (Slang) An American.

**KKB** *Kanya-kanyang bayad* or Dutch treat.

*Kapal* (Slang) Refers to someone who is pushy or who is insensitive to proper behaviour.

*Katulong* (1) Helper; (2) maid.

*Kiping* Fiesta decor of coloured rice wafers, in Quezon Province.

*Kiri* (Slang, vulgar) Mistress.

*Kulam* Bewitchment, sorcery.

*Kulasisi* (Slang, vulgar) Mistress.

*Kuya* Brother.

*Labendera* Washerwoman.

*Lagay* Bribe.

*Lechon* Roast whole suckling pig, specially prepared and cooked over a spit.

*Lihi* An obsessive craving associated with pregnant women.

*Lista sa tubig* (Idiom) Scoring a freebie.

*Lola* Grandmother.

*Lolo* Grandfather.

*Loob* Inner self, as opposed to public image.

*Lumbanog* Distilled coconut spirits.

*Maganda* Beautiful.

*Magpapaalam* To bid goodbye to your hosts as a form of etiquette.

*Mahina* Weak, reference to inability to obtain one's ends through power or political influence.

**Malacañang Palace** Official residence of the President and his/her family.

*Malakas*  Strong, reference to being influential with the powers that be.

*Manananggal*  Female vampire.

*Mangkukulam*  Witch doctor; sorcerer; person believed to have the power to cast evil spells on other people.

*Mano po*  Traditional form of greeting an older person; the hand of the older person is taken by the younger person and touched to the latter's forehead while saying '*mano po*', as a sign of respect.

*Masama*  Bad.

*Mata*  (Sp.) Spanish word for that which kills.

*Mayordoma*  Head housekeeper.

**Meralco**  Manila Electric Company.

*Merienda*  An afternoon snack taken about 4 p.m.

*Merienda-cena*  Party held late in the afternoon where heavier snacks are served, more like an informal dinner party.

**Moriones**  Festival held on the island of Marinduque during Lent.

**Moro-moro**  Folk play depicting a battle between the Christians and the Moors.

*Mukha*  Face.

**NAWASA**  National Water and Sewerage Authority.

*Nazareno*  Nazarene, the Christ; the patron saint of Manila's Quiapo District.

*Ninang*  Godmother.

*Ningas kugon*  Idiomatic expression used to refer to initial enthusiasm for a project that dies out quickly.

*Ninong*  Godfather.

*Nuno sa punso*  Folkloric creature, a tiny old man who lives on an anthill and can cause you good or ill fortune.

*Okay lang*  (Colloquial) Understatement for '(I'm) fine.'

*Oro*  (Sp.) Gold.

*Pabalatbunga*  False front; hypocritical.

*Pabalot*  Doggie-bag.

*Pabaon* Gift of money given to someone about to travel abroad.

*Pabitin* Hangings consisting of candies, sweets and toys for fiesta revellers to reach for and grab.

*Pabongga* Flashy; self-conscious effort to make a spectacular presentation.

**Pahiyas** Fiesta held in Sariaya in honour of San Isidro Labrador, the patron saint of farmers.

*Pakikisama* Getting along with others.

*Pakitang tao* Hypocritical; public image.

*Pakulo* Scheme with a gimmick, designed to impress.

*Palabas* Show; programme.

*Palakasan* Competing for a position for financial or political advantage through the influence of friends in high places (see *mahina* and *malakas*).

*Palay* (1) Unhusked grain, usually of rice, but applicable also to other grains with husk, as wheat; (2) rice plant.

*Palengke* Public market.

*Palo sebo* Game whose object is to obtain a prize at the top of a greased pole by climbing the pole with bare hands and bare feet.

*Panata* Vow; religious promise.

*Pansit* Popular noodle dish.

*Papel* (1) Paper; (2) reputation, influence—*basang papel*, bad or undesirable record; (3) role in a play; (4) (slang) to 'crawl' to someone in order to obtain something from him.

*Pare* (Colloquial) Mate; used to address a fellow man.

*Parol* Christmas lantern.

*Pasalubong* Gift from a traveller, usually some souvenir from one of the places visited.

*Pasiklab* Self-conscious effort to make a spectacular presentation. See also *pabongga*.

*Pastillas* Sweet made from carabao's milk.

*Pasyon* Religious reading of the passion play.

*Patawarin po* 'Forgive me sir/madam', reply to beggars.

**PCVs** Peace Corps volunteers.

**Peacetime** Reference to pre-war days.

*Pinoy* (Slang) A Filipino.

*Pipilitin ko* (Idiom) 'I will try very hard' (literal translation, 'I will force it').

*Plata* (Sp.) Silver.

*Po, ho* Interjection used when speaking to elders or superior to show respect.

**Poise** (Colloquial) One's image of confidence in social situations.

*Porma* Artificially formal (in dress and manner).

*Postura* Attractively dressed.

**PX goods** Refers to commercial goods from military bases sold on the black market.

*Querida* (Sp.) Mistress.

*Reina* Queen.

*Rigodon* Quadrille (dance).

*Sabog* Coin shower.

*Sagala* Maiden in costume in the Lenten procession.

*Sala* Living room.

*Salo-salo* Informal get-together where light meals are served.

*Salubong* (1) Reception; (2) person or group of persons commissioned to meet or receive someone coming or arriving; (3) Lenten ceremony performed on Easter Sunday.

*Santakruzan* Quasi-religious ceremony performed in May.

**Santo Niño** Image of the Holy Child.

*Saya* Long skirt.

*Senakulo* Religious pageant or folk play.

*Señorita* Address used by household help for their female employers.

*Señorito* Address used by household help for their male employers.

*Sige* Go ahead; proceed.

*Siguro* Maybe.

*Sinkil* Muslim bamboo pole dance.

*Sisikapin po* 'I will try.'

**Stateside** From the United States of America.

*Suki* Relationship formed between a vendor and regular customer where the customer patronizes the vendor's shop and in turn is assured of good service and a good bargain; both parties are called *suki*.

*Talunan* Special dish prepared from the rooster that lost a cockfight.

*Tampo* To sulk; (adj.) *matampuhin*—sulky, easily aroused to sulk.

*Tao* Human being, person, mankind.

*Tayo* Pronoun 'we' used when the person addressed is included; a third person may or may not be included; compare with *kami*.

*Tingi* Selling at retail at the smallest unit, e.g. a stick of cigarette.

*Tinikling* Rural folk dance using bamboo poles.

*Tita* Auntie.

*Titignan natin* 'We'll see ...' (... what happens, if we can do it), could imply 'no'.

*Tito* Uncle.

*Tong* Bribe; originally a percentage commission collected from winnings as a fee for the gambling house.

*Trepang* Sea cucumber.

*Tukayo* Someone with the same first name as yourself is your *tukayo*.

**Turrumba** Town fiesta of Pakil, Laguna.

**TY** (Slang) Thank you, meaning a freebie.

*Utang na loob* Debt of gratitude.

**Village** Privately developed suburban residential area, e.g. Magallanes Village, Dasmarines Village, Forbes Park.

*Walang-hiya* (Slang, vulgar) Without shame.

*Yaya* Nanny.

*Zarzuela* Musical play.

# CALENDAR OF FESTIVALS
# AND HOLIDAYS

## JANUARY

### New Year's Day

New Year's Day is celebrated on January 1, and is a public holiday. Good luck for the new year is heralded by bringing gifts to patrons, clients and friends.

### Feast of the Three Kings

Children receive gifts from the Three Wise Men from Bethlehem (their parents of course). This ritual marks the end of the Christmas holidays and is celebrated on the nearest Sunday from January 6.

### Feast of the famous 'Black Nazarene' in Quiapo, Manila

On January 9, Manila's macho proletariat devotees flock to Quiapo Church and then take to the main streets of Quiapo, jostling and scrambling to shoulder the carriage holding the life-sized image of the Black Nazarene.

### Feast of the Santo Niño

The fiesta is celebrated on the third Sunday of the month and is called sinulog in Cebu, marked by peculiar dance steps (sinulog) honouring 'Pit Señor' in the city's main streets.

It is also Ati-atihan time in Kalibo, Aklan (Panay) á la mardi gras. Originally the feast commemorated a peace treaty between indigenous Atis and Malay settlers, but the Aklanons have given it a Christian façade by adopting the image of the Santo Niño as the town's patron saint. For three days and nights (culminating on the third Sunday) Kalibo's streets reverberate with the pounding of drums, the dancing of thousands of outrageously costumed revellers and their cries of "Viva Santo Niño!" Alternatively, visit the town of

Ibajay 30 kilometers from Kalibo during the last week of January for a more authentic and less commercial ati-atihan.

**Chinese New Year**

Chinese New Year is celebrated sometime within January 21 and February 19 with popping firecrackers, dragon dances and large signs emblazoned with: Kong Hei Fat Choy!

# FEBRUARY

**Feast of Our Lady of Candelaria**

A major religious event in the Visayas, especially in Jaro, Iloilo, and is celebrated on February 2.

**People Power Day**

Public holiday on February 25 commemorating the 1986 historic event at EDSA (Epifanio de los Santos Avenue) when people power faced down tanks and armed soldiers to bring down the dictatorship of Ferdinand Marcos.

# MARCH–APRIL

**Religious Lenten period**

Public holidays on Maunday Thursday, Good Friday and Easter Sunday. The more devout frown upon boisterous behaviour, travel or even bathing during Lenten. Usual solemn rituals in church are the 'washing of the feet', 'stations of the cross' and 'seven last words'.

In San Fernando, Pampanga and some neighbouring towns of Manila, Christ's crucifixion is reenacted literally, and some over-zealous devotees are happy to have themselves actually nailed to a cross. Self-flagellation is also a common religious ritual.

The salubong is performedEarly Easter Sunday (Domingo de ramos) in traditional-minded towns throughout the archipelago. The images of Christ and that of the Blessed Mother are taken from the Church in procession on opposite routes to meet at the plaza under a bunting-decorated bamboo arch.

## *MAY*

Through this month of flowers, many small communities hold a Santa Cruzan procession commemorating St. Helena's search for the Holy Cross.

### *Feast of San Isidro Labrador, the patron saint of farmers*

On May 15, the towns of Lukban and Sariyaya in Quezon Province, are decked with agricultural produce (Pahiyas) to honour the patron saint of peasants in anticipation of rain and bountiful harvests. In Pulilan Bulacan, Angono Rizal, and San Isidro, Nueva Ecija it is the day of the carabao: the farmer's four-legged helper is decked with flowers and led in processions, followed by carabao races.

## *JUNE*

### *Independence Day*

Public holiday on June 12. The usual parades and speeches.

### *Feast of St. John the Baptist*

On June 24, merrymakers douse (baptize) unsuspecting passers-by in Metro Manila's San Juan district.

## *JULY*

On the first Sunday of July in Bocaue, Bulacan, a fiesta, celebrating the slaying of a crocodile that threatened the duck-egg center of Pateros is held on the last gasp of Pasig River in Pateros.

## *AUGUST*

The only significant festival is held over two weeks in Davao City involving tribal performances and flower and food exhibits.

## *SEPTEMBER*

The feast of the Blessed Virgin of Peñafrancia held on the third Sunday of this month in Naga is an important religious water procession for the people of Bicol.

## OCTOBER

### Feast of Nuestra Señora del Pilar, Zamboanga City's patron saint

The second Sunday of the month is also La Naval commemorating a victorious naval battle on October 3, 1646 led by Nuestra Señora del Rosario between Spanish vessels and a Dutch armada off Manila Bay's Corregidor Island. La Naval is also commemorated on the last Sunday of the month in Angeles City, Pampanga.

### MasKara festival in Bacolod City

A decorous mardi gras affair celebrated on October 19.

## NOVEMBER

### All Saints Day

Public holiday on November 1. A time to remember the dead as this day is inter-linked with the following day ( All Souls Day). People keep vigil over the tombs of their departed kin and friends. The solemn ritual borders on the festive with flowers for the graves and food for themselves and guests. People play mahjong or watch TV on portable sets as they keep the long vigil.

### Feast of San Clemente

The town of Angono in Rizal province celebrates the day of its patron saint on November 23 with a land and water procession on the lake.

### Bonifacio Day (National Heroes Day)

Public holiday on November 30. This day used to commemorate all heroes but now focus on Andres Bonifacio, the revolutionary who headed the Katipunan, the organization which set off the armed uprising against Spain in 1896, at the expense of countless other heroes.

## DECEMBER

### Feast of our Lady of the Immaculate Conception

In the old fishing town of Malabon, a water festival is held from Malabon River to Manila Bay. Older Filipinos remember with sorrow

245

December 8 as the day Japanese planes bombed Manila and Clark Field starting World War II here.

### Misa de Gallo or Simbang Gabi

Nine early dawn masses before Christmas are celebrated from December 16–25, although the Christmas carols over the air waves and department stores can be heard from November. After attending early morning mass, devotees feast on hot salabat (ginger tea) and freshly baked bibingka (rice cake) sold in in stalls outside the church.

### Panunuluyan ritual in Valencia, Bulacan

A quasi-religious pageant celebrated on December 24 in which a couple from the community reenact Joseph and Mary's search for a room in Bethlehem.

### Christmas Day

Public holiday on December 25. Presents and feasting mark the day. Everyone is remembered in the gift giving, including hired help, the postman and local policemen, firemen, and the garbage collectors along with all the little children.

### Feast of the Holy Innocents

December 28 is a day to pull harmless pranks on the innocent. Don't succumb should a friend ask you for the loan of a small amount of money.

### Rizal Day

Public holiday on December 30. Instead of celebrating the national hero's birthday (June 19) Filipinos celebrate the day he was shot by a firing squad on Luneta (now Rizal Park) this fateful day in 1896.

### New Year's Eve

Decembe 31 is a nightmare for emergency rooms in hospitals deluged with firecracker casualties. New Year's Eve celebrations in the Philippines, with liquor-laced revellers flinging casually manufactured, lethal fireworks with wild abandon, is boisterous and hazardous, what with the occasional trigger-happy soldier or policeman firing his pistol into the night sky.

# RESOURCE GUIDE

## HEALTH AND EMERGENCY

Some major hospitals in the **Metro Manila** area are:
**Makati Medical Center** 2 Amorsolo St., Legaspi Village, Makati. Tel 815 9911/892 5544. **Cardinal Santos Medical Center** Wilson St. Greenhills, San Juan Metro Manila Tel 726 3410 11. **Manila Medical Center** 1122 General Luna St. Ermita Manila Tel 591661. **Manila Doctors Hospital** 667 United Nations Ave. Ermita Manila Tel 503011. **San Juan de Dios Hospital** 2772 Roxas Blvd. Pasay City Tel 831 9731 36.

In **Cebu**:
**Cebu Doctors Hospital** Osmeña Boulevard Tel 253 751

For general emergencies:
**Tourist Assistance Unit (TAU)** TM Kalaw St. Rizal Park Ermita, Manila Tel 501 728/501 660 (24 hour service). **Emergency Police** 166. **Information** 114.

## HOME AND FAMILY

These hotels fall in the price range of P150–P600 per night (some of these offer single-sex dormitory accommodation):
**Manila International Youth Hostel** 4227-9 Tomas Claudio St. **Paranaque** Tel (02) 832 0680. **New Casa Pensionne** Corner of Pedro Gil and Leon Ginto Sts. **Ermita** Tel (02) 522 1740. **Pension Filipina** 572 Engracia Reyes St. Ermita Tel (02) 521 1488. **Richmond Pension** 1165 Grey St. Ermita Tel (02) 525 3864. **Soledad Pension House** 1529 Mabini St. Malate Tel (02) 524 0706.

Hotels in the price range of P1000-P3000 per night:
**Bianca's Garden Hotel** 2139 Adriatico St. Malate Tel (02) 526 0351. **Copa Businessman's Hotel** 912 Arnaiz Ave. Makati Tel (02) 844

8811. **Hotel Soriente** 545 A Flores St. Ermita Tel (02) 523 9456.
**Park Hotel** 1032 Belen St. Paco Tel (02) 521-2371.

## Taxes
The rate of individual income tax is progressive and ranges from 10%
to 32% of gross income. Corporate tax is 32%. There is a value added
tax on goods and services.

## ENTERTAINMENT AND LEISURE
### Filipino Food
**Kamayan** Padre Faura St. Ermita. **Barrio Fiesta** Makati Avenue
Makati/United Nations Avenue Ermita. **Zamboanga Restaurant**
Adriatico St. Makati. **Patio Mequeni** Remedios St. Malate.
**Josephine's** Roxas Blvd. Pasay City. **Aristocrat** Roxas Blvd. Malate.

### Nightspots
**Cats** International Hotel Arnais Ave. Makati. **Strumm's** Greenbelt
Square Makati. **Zu** Shangri-La Hotel, Makati Ave. Makati. **Stardust**
Quezon Ave./Timog Ave. Quezon City. Expect to pay a cover charge
and/or table charge.

### For Bookworms
**National Bookstore** (major shopping malls). **La Solidaridad Book
Shop** Padre Faura St. Ermita. **The Filipino Book Shop** Glorietta
shopping Mall in Makati. If you see a book published in the Philippines
that interests you, it is best to buy it at once, because print runs are
small and few books enjoy a reprint much less a second edition.

### Libraries
**The National Library** T.M. Kalaw St. Ermita. **The Lopez Memorial
Museum** Pasig Metro Manila. **The Ayala Museum Library** in
Makati.

## *Cultural Organizations*

Most cultural organizations are linked to the **National Council for Culture and the Arts (NCCA)**.

### *Museums*

**The National Museum** at the Rizal Park on Burgos Street offers the best archeological display of the Philippines' prehistoric past going back to the Neolothic Age. **The Ayala Museum**, on Makati Avenue, Makati, features 60 dioramas covering high points of Philippine history from the prehispanic to the 1986 people power triumph at EDSA. **The Chinoy Museum** in Intramuros features the Chinese heritage of Filipinos through life-sized dioramas reconstructing the life style of the Chinese in the nineteenth century as well as large sized vintage photographs. On one side of San Agustin Church in Intramuros is the **San Agustin Museum** housing religious icons and vestments of the Spanish period. **Casa Manila** on General Luna St., Intramuros, is a restored house with a courtyard recreating an amalgam of the architecture and lifestyle of the Spanish Period. Antique shops and a restaurant form part of the complex. **The Lopez Memorial Museum** on the ground floor of the Chronicle Building on Meralco Avenue, Pasig, houses more than 13,000 books on the Philippines, many of them rare and out-of-print. Kids will enjoy **Museo Pambata**, a children's museum on Roxas Blvd. Ermita.

### *Theatres*

**The William Shaw Theater** Fifth floor Shangri-La Plaza Mall EDSA. **Mandaluyong** Tel (02) 633 4821. **The Cultural Center of the Philippines (CCP)** Roxas Blvd. Malate Tel (02) 832 3878. **The Folk Arts Theater** CCP Complex Roxas Blvd. Malate Tel (02) 832 1120.

### *Music and Dance*

**Paco Park** Chamber music concerts on Friday evenings at 6 p.m.

**Puerto Real** On Saturdays at 6 p.m. **Rizal Park** Concert at the Park on Sundays at 5 p.m. Ballroom dancing is highly popular among upper-middle class Filipinos. An interesting feature is the 'DI', or dance instructor, who will dance with you all night for a generous fee. DI fees range from several thousand pesos a night to P300.

## COMMUNICATIONS

For international calls dial 00, the country code, the local code, and the telephone number or ask the **international operator** for help (108). **Domestic operator** 109. **Directory assistance for Manila** 114. **Directory assistance for areas outside Manila** 112.

### Travelling by Bus

The main bus companies in Manila are:

**Autobus Transport Systems** Corner of Dimasalang and Laong Laan Sts. Sampaloc Tel (02) 743 6870. **BLTB** EDSA Pasay City Tel (02) 833 5501. **Dagupan Bus Company** Corner of EDSA and New York St. Cubao Quezon City Tel (02) 727 2330. **Dangwa Tranco** 1600 Dimasalang St. Sampaloc Tel (02) 731 2859. **Gold Line Tours** Corner of MH Del Pilar and Pedro Gil Sts. Malate Tel (02) 450 0506. **JAC Liner** Taft Ave. Pasay City Tel (02) 831 8977. **JB Bicol Express Line** Aurora Blvd. Pasay City Tel (02) 833 2950. **Peñafrancia Tours** 483 Pedro Gil St. Malate Tel (02) 450 1122. **Philtranco** Alimall Araneta Center EDSA Cubao Quezon City Tel (02) 925 1759. **Tritran** 2124 Taft Ave. Pasay City Tel (02) 831-4700. **Victory Liner** 713 Rizal Ave. Extension Caloocan City Tel (02) 361 1506.

### Travelling by Train

The **LRT (Light Rail Transit)** runs from Baclaran in Pasay City to Monumento in Caloocan City. The **EDSA** takes you from Pasay (linked to the first railway system) to Quezon City. Tokens cost 10 pesos and can be used for one ride to any stop. The LRT runs from 5:30

a.m. to 10:30 p.m. daily except Good Friday. There is no reliable rail system for travel outside Manila. Take buses instead.

## Taxis and Jeepneys

The official flag-down rate is 20 pesos and then 5 pesos for every kilometre travelled. Some of the large hotels also have their own taxis or use a company called Hotaxco that hire taxis out for the day. There are no set stops for jeepneys. Flag them down anywhere and simply yell out 'Para!' (stop) when you want to.

## MEDIA

### Newspapers and Magazines

The major **newspapers in English** are: *Business World*; *Manila Bulletin*; *Philippine Daily Enquirer*; *Philippine Post*; *The Philippine Star*; *Village Voice*. **Magazine** available include: *Agenda Online* (Philippine entertainment scene); *Agham Science Magazine*; *Arts and Artists*; *Computerworld Philippines*; *Food & Beverage Magazine*; *PC World*; *Pen & Ink* (Philippine literary journal); *The Philippine Diver*; *Journalism Review* (special forum for the press and media); *Philippine Panorama* (Sunday newsmagazine of the *Manila Bulletin*).

## GENERAL COUNTRY INFORMATION

### Appliances and Utilities

The electricity voltage used in most parts of the Philippines is 220V. In Baguio the voltage is 110V. Metro Manila carries both. Electrical sockets are designed to take plugs with two straight prongs.

### Pre-Entry Vaccinations

The following vaccinations should be considered: Diphtheria; tetanus; hepatitis A and B; Japanese B encephalitis; tuberculosis; cholera; typhoid; polio; rabies. Check with your doctor. Malaria medication is advised if you plan to travel to outlying areas. If you are travelling from parts of Africa and South America, you will be legally required to have a yellow fever vaccine before entering the Philippines.

## Embassies

**Australia** Ground Floor Doña Salustiana Ty Tower 104 Paseo de Roxas Legaspi Village Makati Tel (02) 750 2850. **Canada** Ninth Floor Allied Bank Bldg. Ayala Ave. Makati. Tel (02) 810 8749/8861. **China** 149 Roxas Blvd. Parañaque Tel (02) 879 8020. **France** 16th Floor Pacific Star Bldg. Gil Puyat Ave. Makati. Tel (02) 810 1981. **Germany** 6th Floor Solid Bank Bldg. 777 Paseo de Roxas, Salcedo Village Makati Tel (02) 892 4906. **Japan** 2627 Roxas Blvd. Pasay City Tel (02) 551 5710. **USA** 1201 Roxas Blvd. Ermita Tel (02) 523 1001. **UK** 18th Floor LV Locsin Bldg. Makati Tel (02) 816 7116.

## General and Tourist Bureaus and Websites

**Department of Tourism (DOT)** DOT Building TM Kalaw St. Ermita, Manila Tel (02) 524 1703
**Useful websites**: www.filipinolinks.com. www.diyaryo.com. www.philtourism.com

## Immigration, Residency and Nationality Issues

Stays up to 21 days do not require a visa. You can apply for a 59-day stay or extend your 21-day stay to a 59-day stay. For a longer stay, you will need to speak to the Filipino Consulate in your country or deal with the local immigration office in the Philippines.

## Country Statistics (1999 estimate)

**Population:** 79,345,812, 37% under 15 years of age, 4% over 65 years. Population growth rate: 2.04%. **Ethnic groups:** Christian Malay 91.5%, Muslim Malay 4%, Chinese 1.5%, other 3%. **Religions:** Roman Catholic 83%, Protestant 9%, Muslim 5%, Buddhist and other 3%. **Industries:** textiles, pharmaceuticals, chemicals, wood products, food processing, electronics assembly, petroleum refining, fishing.

**Agriculture products:** rice, coconuts, corn, sugar cane, bananas, pineapples, mangoes, pork, eggs, beef, fish.

## BUSINESS INFORMATION

Foreigners are not permitted to engage in the following: mass media; services involving practice of licensed professions, cooperatives; private security agencies; small scale mining; utilization of marine resources within archipelagic waters, territorial sea and exclusive economic zones; the ownership, management, and operation of cockpits; manufacture repair, stockpiling and/or distribution of nuclear weapons; manufacture repair, stockpiling and/or distribution of biological/chemical/radiological weapons.

Foreign companies can own 100% equity if the business is located in the special economic zones, otherwise at least 70% of production must be for export. To enjoy 100% foreign equity when 100% of the production is sold to the domestic market, the foreign capital equity must be at least US$150,000 or US$100,000 should the company bring in new technology or employ at least 50 Filipino workers.

All remmitances of foreign exchange must be registered with the Central Bank of the Philippines. You can file an application with the Bureau of Investments (BOI) for investment incentives if your business venture qualifies under the Investment Priorities Plan (IPP). Otherwise, register the articles of partnership or incorporation with the Securities and Exchange Commission (SEC) Those businesses located in specific economic zones could also try registering directly with the Philippine Economic Zone Authority (PEZA). Single proprietors should register with the Domestic Trade and Regulation and Consumer Protection (DTRCP).

### Legal Aid Agencies

**www.legalground.com** provides free legal services, information and advice 24 hours. **www.philtaxlaws.com** gives the most comprehensive Philippine tax related information.

# BIBLIOGRAPHY

Agoncillo, T. & Alfonso, O., *History of the Filipino People*, Quezon City: Malaya Books, 1967.

Andres, T.D., *Understanding Filipino Values. A Management Approach*, Quezon City: New Day Publishers, 1981.

Arce, W.F. & Poblador, N.S., 'Formal Organizations in the Philippines: Motivation, Behaviour, Structure and Change', in M.R. Hollnsteiner (Ed.), *Society, Culture and the Filipino*, Quezon City: Institute of Philippine Culture, Ateneo de Manila University, 1979.

Blair, E.H. & Robertson, J.A., *The Philippine Islands, 1493–1898*, 55 volumes, Cleveland, Ohio: Arthur H. Clark, 1903–09.

Bulatao, J., SJ, *Split-level Christianity*, Manila: U.S.T. Press, 1966.

Coates, A., *Rizal: Philippine Nationalist and Martyr*, Hongkong: Oxford University Press, 1968.

Daigler, G.M., *Living in the Philippines*, Makati: The American Chamber of Commerce of the Philippines, 1980.

Doherty, J.F., SJ, 'Who Controls the Economy: Some Need Not Try as Hard as Others', in B.A. Aquino (Ed.), *Cronies and Enemies: The Current Philippine Scene*, Philippine Studies Occasional Paper No. 5, Honolulu: University of Hawaii, 1982.

Fox, R., *Area Handbook on the Philippines*, Vol. 1, Chapters l–VIII, HRAF, The University of Chicago, 1956.

Guthrie, G.M. (Ed.), *Six Perspectives on the Philippines*, Manila: Bookmark, 1968.

Guthrie, G.M. & Jimenez-Jacobs, P., *Child-rearing and Personality Development in the Philippines*, Manila: Bookmark, 1967.

Hollnsteiner, M.R., *The Dynamics of Power in a Philippine*

*Municipality*, Community Development Research Council, University of the Philippines, 1963.

Hollnsteiner, M.R. 'Reciprocity in the Lowland Philippines', *IPC Papers No. 1*, Quezon City: Ateneo de Manila University, 1961.

Hollnsteiner, M.R. (Ed.), *Society, Culture and the Filipino*, Quezon City: Institute of Philippine Culture, Ateneo de Manila University, 1979.

Koehler, G. 'Personality Needs of German Wives and Satisfaction with Life in the Philippines', Unpublished thesis, 1979.

Lapuz, L.V., *A Study of Psychopathology*, Quezon City: University of the Philippines Press, 1973.

Lapuz, L.V., *Filipino Marriages in Crisis*, Quezon City: New Day Publishers, 1977.

Lynch, F., SJ, 'Philippine Values II: Social Acceptance', *Philippine Studies*, Vol. 10, No. 1 (January 1962), 82–99.

Lynch, F., SJ, 'Town fiesta: An Anthropologist's View', *Philippines International*, Vol. 6, No. 6, 4–11, 26–27.

Rizal, J., *El Filibusterismo*, Manila: Community Publishers, Inc., 1961.

Rizal, J., *Noli me Tangere*, Manila: Community Publishers, Inc., 1961.

Roces, A. (Ed.), *Filipino Heritage. The Making of a Nation*, Vols. 1–10, Manila: Lahing Pilipino Publishing Inc., 1978.

Roces, A.R., *Fiesta*, Quezon City: Vera-Reyes Inc., 1980.

Szanton, D.L., 'Cultural Confrontation in the Philippines', in R.B. Textor (Ed.), *Cultural Frontiers of the Peace Corps*, Cambridge: MIT Press, 1966.

Wolff, L., *Little Brown Brother*, New York: Doubleday & Co., Inc., 1961.

# LABOUR AND BUSINESS

Employment of Househelpers (Labour Code, 1978)

**Section 1. General statement on coverage.**

(a) The provision of this Rule shall apply to all househelpers whether employed on full or part-time basis.

(b) The term 'househelper' as used herein is synonymous to the term 'domestic servant' and shall refer to any person, whether male or female, who renders services in and about the employer's home and which services are usually necessary or desirable for the maintenance and enjoyment thereof, and ministers exclusively to the personal comfort and enjoyment of the employer's family.

**Section 2. Method of payment not determinant.**

The provisions of this Rule shall apply irrespective of the method of payment of wages agreed upon by the employer and househelper, whether it be hourly, daily, weekly, or monthly, or in piece or output basis.

**Section 3. Children of househelpers.**

The children and relatives of househelpers who live under the employer's roof and who share the accommodations provided for the househelpers by the employer, shall not be deemed as househelpers if they are not otherwise engaged as such are not required to perform any substantial household work.

**Section 4. Employment contract.**

The initial contract for household service shall not last for more than two years. However, such contract may be renewed from year to year.

**Section 5. Minimum monthly wage.**

The minimum compensation of househelpers should not be less than the following rates:

(a) 60 pesos a month for those employed in the cities of Manila,

Quezon, Pasay, and Caloocan, and in the municipalities of Makati, San Juan, Mandaluyong, Muntinlupa, Navotas, Malabon, Parañaque, Las Piñas, Pasig, and Marikina, in the Province of Rizal.

(b) 45 pesos a month for those employed in other chartered cities and first class municipalities, and

(c) 30 pesos a month for those in other municipalities.

[Note: Changing economic situation requires a check on current rates.]

## Section 6. Equivalent daily rate.

The equivalent minimum daily wage rate of househelper shall be determined by dividing the applicable minimum monthly rate by 30 days.

## Section 7. Payment by results.

Where the method of payment of wages agreed upon by the employer and the househelper is on piece or output basis, the piece or output rate shall be such as will assure the househelper of the minimum monthly or the equivalent daily rate as provided in this issuance.

## Section 8. Minimum cash wage.

The minimum wage rate prescribed under this Rule shall be basic cash wages which shall be paid to the househelpers in addition to lodging, food, and medical attendance.

## Section 9. Time and manner of payment.

Wages shall be paid directly to the househelper to whom they are due at least once a month. No deductions therefrom shall be made by the employer unless authorized by the househelper himself or by any existing law.

## Section 10. Assignment to non-household work.

No househelper be assigned to work in a commercial, industrial or agricultural enterprise at a wage or salary rate lower than that provided for agricultural and non-agricultural workers.

## Section 11. Opportunity for education.

If the househelper is under the age of 18 years, the employer shall give him or her an opportunity for at least elementary education. The cost of such education shall be part of the househelper's compensation, unless there is a stipulation to the contrary.

### Section 12. Treatment of househelper.

The employer shall treat the househelper in a just and humane manner. In no case shall physical violence be used upon the househelper.

### Section 13. Board, lodging, and medical attendance.

The employer shall furnish the househelper, free of charge, suitable and sanitary living quarters, as well as adequate food and medical attendance.

### Section 14. Indemnity for unjust termination of service.

If the period for household service is fixed, neither the employer nor the househelper may terminate the contract before the expiration of these regulations is higher than that prescribed in the Code and in this issuance, the same shall not be reduced or diminished by the employer on or after said date.

If the househelper leaves without justified reason, he or she shall forfeit any unpaid salary due him or her not exceeding 15 days.

### Section 15. Employment certification.

Upon the severance of the household service relationship, the househelper may demand from the employer, a written statement of the nature and duration of the service and his or her efficiency and conduct as househelper.

### Section 16. Funeral expenses.

In case of death of the household helper the employer shall bear the funeral expenses commensurate to the standards of life of the deceased.

### Section 17. Disposition of househelper's body.

Unless so desired by the househelper or by his or her guardian with court approval, the transfer or use of the body of a deceased househelper for purposes other than burial is prohibited. When so authorized by the househelper, the transfer, use and disposltion of the body shall be in accordance with the provision of Republic Act 349.

## Section 18. Employment records.

The employer may keep such records as he may deem necessary to reflect the actual terms and conditions of employment of his househelper which the latter shall authenticate by signature or thumbmark upon request of the employer.

## Section 19. Prohibited reduction of pay.

When the compensation of the househelper before the promulgation of these regulations is higher than that prescribed in the Code and in this issuance, the same shall not be reduced or diminished by the employer on or after said date.

## Section 20. Relation to other laws and agreements.

Nothing in these rules and regulations shall deprive a househelper of the right to seek higher wages, shorter working hours and better working conditions than those prescribed herein, and should not justify an employer in reducing any benefit or privilege granted to the househelper under existing laws, agreements or voluntary employer practices, with terms more favourable to the househelper than those prescribed in this Rule.


## *The Nationalist Business Credo (1986 Constitution)*

Enshrined in the post-Marcos 1986 constitution are these pertinent passages:

### State policies

The State shall develop a self-reliant and an independent national economy effectively controlled by Filipinos. (Sec. 19)

### Article XII. National economy and patrimony

...The State shall protect Filipino enterprises against unfair foreign competition and trade practices. (Sec. 1)

The State shall protect the nation's marine wealth in its archipelagic waters, territorial sea, and exclusive economic zone, and reserve its use and enjoyment exclusively to Filipino citizens. (Sec. 2)

The President may enter into agreements with foreign-owned corporations involving either technical or financial assistance for large-scale exploration, development, and utilization of minerals, petroleum, and other mineral oils according to the general terms and conditions provided by law, based on real contributions to the economic growth and general welfare of the country. In such agreements, the Senate shall promote the development and use of local scientific and technical resources. (Sec. 2)

The Congress shall, upon recommendation of the economic and planning agency, when the national interests dictates, reserve to citizens of the Philippines or to corporations or associations at least sixty per centum of whose capital is owned by such citizens, or such higher percentage as Congress may prescribe, certain areas of investments. The Congress shall enact measures that will encourage the formation and operation of enterprises whose capital is wholly owned by Filipinos. In the grant of rights, privileges, and concessions covering the national economy and patrimony, the State shall give preference to qualified Filipinos. (Sec. 10)

No franchise, certificates or any other form of authorization for the operation of a public utility shall be granted except to citizens of the Philippines or to corporations or associations organized under the laws of the Philippines at least sixty per centum of whose capital is owned by such citizens... The participation of foreign investors in the governing body of any public utility enterprise shall be limited to their proportionate share in its capital, and all the executive and managing officers of such corporation or association must be citizens of the Philippines. (Sec. 11)

The State shall promote the preferential use of Filipino labour, domestic materials and locally produced goods, and adopt measures that help make them competitive. (Sec. 12)

The practice of all professions in the Philippines shall be limited to Filipino citizens, save in cases prescribed by law. (Sec. 14)

Article XIV. Education, Science and Technology, Arts, Culture and Sports:

**Education:** (2) Educational institutions, other than those established by religious group or mission boards, shall be owned solely by citizens of the Philippines or corporations or associations at least sixty per centum of the capital of which is owned by such citizens. The Congress may, however, require increased Filipino equity participation in all educational institutions. The control and administration of educational institutions shall be vested in citizens of the Philippines. No educational institution shall be established exclusively for aliens and no group of aliens shall comprise more than one-third of the enrolment in any school. The provisions of this sanction shall not apply to schools established for foreign diplomatic personnel and their dependants and, unless otherwise provided by law, for any other foreign temporary residents. (Sec. 2)

**General Provisions** (1) The ownership and management of mass media shall be limited to citizens of the Philippines, or to corporations, cooperatives or associations, wholly owned and managed by such citizens. (Sec. 2)

# THE AUTHORS

Now based in Sydney, Australia, freelance writer-painter **Alfredo Roces** was editor of *GEO*, Australasia's Geographical Magazine, from 1978 to 1991. A Filipino, he served as editor-in-chief of a ten-volume study on Philippine culture and history entitled *Filipino Heritage* (1978), now in its second printing. He was a daily columnist for the country's leading newspaper, *The Manila Times*, for more than ten years, for which he gained a Columnist of the Year Award from the Citizens Council for Mass Media in 1971. Earlier he was cited as one of Ten Outstanding Young Men (TOYM) in 1961 for his contribution to the study of Philippine Culture.

An artist with a Bachelor of Fine Arts from the University of Notre Dame in the USA, he authored various books: *The Story of the Philippines* (MacCormic Mathers, 1968); *Amorsolo* (Filipinas Foundation, 1975); *Sanso* (Filcapital Development Corporation General Bank and Trust Co, 1976); *Filipino Nude* (Infinity Inc. Vera Reyes Press, 1977); *Drawings* (Infinity Inc., 1974).

 **Grace Roces** has a Bachelor of Arts Honours Degree in Psychology from the University of Sydney. She is currently a design consultant for Wespac Training. Grace grew up in Manila and moved to Australia with her co-author father and family in 1978. She is married to Howard Boorman.

# INDEX